THE BRONTËS

CHARLOTTE BRONTË

THE BRONTËS

By FLORA MASSON

KENNIKAT PRESS
Port Washington, N. Y./London

PR
4168
·M37
1970

THE BRONTES

First published in 1912
Reissued in 1970 by Kennikat Press
Library of Congress Catalog Card No: 73-103203
SBN 8046-0840-7

Manufactured by Taylor Publishing Company   Dallas, Texas

CONTENTS

CHAP.		PAGE
I.	THE PARSON AND HIS WIFE	9
II.	HAWORTH	15
III.	THE TRAGEDY OF COWAN BRIDGE	19
IV.	THE BRONTË CHILDREN AT HOME	23
V.	MISS WOOLER'S SCHOOL	28
VI.	THE PRIDE OF THE FAMILY	32
VII.	THE PEN, THE PALETTE, AND THE POET LAUREATE	37
VIII.	"QUALIFIED TO TEACH"	45
IX.	PENSIONNAT HÉGER	53
X.	CURRER, ELLIS, AND ACTON BELL	62
XI.	THE VALLEY OF THE SHADOW	70
XII.	THE ZENITH	78
XIII.	THE PASSING OF CURRER BELL	86
	CHRONOLOGY	91
	REFERENCES	92

THE BRONTËS

CHAPTER I

THE PARSON AND HIS WIFE

THERE is no doubt that the Brontës were a very eccentric family. "Do not underrate her oddity," was the advice given by a friend of Charlotte Brontë to Sir Wemyss Reid when he was writing his *Monograph* of the novelist. But nobody who writes about the Brontës to-day is likely to underrate their oddities: far likelier is it, as literary taste and standards alter with the years, that the Brontë genius will come to be underrated. Are there any people still living to remember the "rush for copies" of *Jane Eyre*, or the intensity of feeling produced by *Villette?* The big sales are to-day of novels of a very different order: Charlotte Brontë and her family have taken their place, once for all, among the literary enthusiasms of a bygone age.

Genius, eccentricity and disease too often, as we know, dwell together; but surely never did they keep closer company than under the roof of that old stone parsonage at Haworth, on the windswept Yorkshire moors. The genius and the eccentricity seem to have come from the Irish, peasant-born father and the line of wild-blooded, rhapsodic Celts behind him. The disease —for the Brontë family was to be riddled by consumption, to live out its days in its generation and become extinct under that same parsonage roof—was the sadder heritage from the gentle little Cornish mother, who never saw Penzance and her own people again after she met and married her handsome Irish curate in the summer of 1812, when she was on a visit to her " uncle, aunt, and Cousin Jane " in Yorkshire.

It is so easy to be wise after the event, to shake one's head over a marriage that took place a hundred years ago, and proved to be not a particularly happy one. If Miss Maria Branwell of Penzance, in that summer of 1812, had said "No" to the Reverend Patrick Brontë, B.A., curate of Hartshead-cum-Clifton, those six little delicate Brontës would not have been brought into the world at the rate of one a year, and left motherless, to toddle hand-in-hand about the Haworth moors. But then, neither would there have been any "Currer, Ellis, and Acton Bell"; there would have been no Brontë novels to be discovered by Messrs. Smith & Elder, no Brontë story to tell, no " Brontë cult."

But Miss Maria Branwell said "Yes"—a demure little yes, but quite audible and firmly spoken; a pathetic little packet of love-letters survives to tell the tale. And in saying that word she sealed her own fate, and earned her own little niche, by contributing one of its most passionately human chapters to the history of our literature.

When the Reverend Patrick Brontë made love to Miss Maria Branwell, he was thirty-five, a B.A. of Cambridge, handsome, clever, eloquent, and very ambitious. Like his famous compatriot, Father O'Flynn, Mr. Brontë had " a way wid 'im," which had already materially smoothed his path in life. One wonders how much he told his Maria about those united parishes of Drumballyroney and Drumgooland, in County Down, and the poor little thatched Irish cabin where he was born, which his parents rented for something like sixpence a week. For Patrick Brontë's parents were very poor people indeed, and Patrick was the eldest of their ten sturdy children. His mother, Alice McClory, a village beauty and a Roman Catholic, had made a runaway Protestant marriage; and Hugh Brunty or Brontee, her husband, was a forceful character, robust and illiterate, a genius in his way, and a kind of celebrity

THE PARSON AND HIS WIFE 11

among his neighbours. When he met Alice McClory, Hugh Brontë was working at a lime-kiln; but after their marriage he seems to have set up a corn-kiln in the kitchen of their cabin, where his beautiful wife also plied her spinning-wheel. Alice McClory's smile, it is said, " would have tamed a mad bull." It was to " Brontë's kiln " the neighbours brought their oats to be roasted, and there also they would gather of nights to listen, by the red glow of the furnace, while Hugh Brontë told his wonderful stories—some of them so weird and blood-curdling that the simple villagers were afraid to go home in the dark.[1]

Patrick Brontë, red-headed, and the eldest of ten, had been brought up a hand-loom weaver; but he was a very clever boy, a staunch young Ulster Protestant, under the village-ban of a "mixed marriage." With the help of Andrew Harshaw, a Presbyterian schoolmaster in the neighbourhood, he had managed to learn some Latin and Greek and a little Euclid. He bought and borrowed books—Milton's *Paradise Lost* among them—and at sixteen " Master Brontë " found himself in the proud position of teacher in the Presbyterian village school at Glascar Hill. On the advice of his Presbyterian friend, he joined the Episcopalians; and a year or two later Mr. Tighe, the rector of Drumgooland, appointed him teacher in his parish school. Not only that—he was engaged to give private lessons to the little Tighes and the children of "another local magnate " in the drawing-room of the Drumgooland rectory; and from the rectory drawing-room it was but a step to the gates of St. John's College, Cambridge.

And so in 1802, at five-and-twenty, Patrick Brontë had said good-bye to Ireland. He did very well at St. John's—gained three exhibitions, and took his B.A. in 1806. And when all England was making ready for Bonaparte and a French invasion, and a university volunteer corps was hurriedly raised at Cambridge, the young Irishman found himself drilling in congenial company, shoulder to shoulder with Lord Palmerston.

[1] Dr. Wright's *The Brontës in Ireland*.

No sooner was he ordained than a curacy was found for him in the little village of Wethersfield, in Essex, his vicar being no less a person than the Cambridge Regius Professor of Civil Law. And at Wethersfield the young Irishman fell in love.

Mary Burder, Patrick Brontë's first love, was the pretty daughter of a well-to-do Essex farmer, lately dead; and she was the niece of the old lady in whose house, just opposite the Norman church with its green copper spire, the new curate had taken up his abode. For a brief space the two young people were in paradise; and then Mary Burder's uncle and guardian, an angry man, came down on them, and carried Mary Burder off, virtually a prisoner, to his own house. The curate's messages and letters were intercepted, and when after a time the girl was allowed to return to Wethersfield, the curate was gone. A little packet of her letters to him was returned to her, from which, when she opened it, there dropped out "a small card, with her lover's face in profile," and—Oh, Patrick, Patrick!—the words beneath it, "Mary, you have torn the heart,—spare the face!"[1]

It is not known whether, when he left Essex in 1809, Patrick Brontë carried his torn heart and handsome face back to Drumballyroney, in County Down. By general report, he never went back to Ireland after he left it in 1802; but there is a local tradition that he did go home, and that he preached at least one sermon in Drumballyroney Church before a full congregation of admiring friends and neighbours—"a gran' sermon, and never had anything in his han' the whole time." However this may be, Patrick Brontë was not a bad son or brother. His first letter from Cambridge had carried with it a half-sovereign under the seal, and so long as his mother lived he managed to send her £20 a year. He kept up occasional correspondence—a little formal and dignified, as befitted his cloth—with his numerous brothers and sisters in County Down. More than once he helped them, and in his solitary old age, when he

[1] Mr. Augustine Birrell's *Charlotte Brontë*.

THE PARSON AND HIS WIFE 13

was making his modest will, he remembered them all.

The rejected suitor found other curacies. In 1811 he was curate of Hartshead-cum-Clifton—" a very handsome fellow, full of Irish enthusiasm, and with something of an Irishman's capability of falling easily in love."[1] He had always been fond of books, especially of poetry. Some of his own verses had been recited by his little pupils in the village school at Drumballyroney. At Hartshead he made a collection of his poems, and the volume, *Cottage Poems*, bound in vellum, was published at Halifax in 1811. But Hartshead knew him not only as a good-looking Irish curate who wrote poetry. Those were troublous times in the West Riding ; "industrial unrest" was abroad then, with a vengeance. Patrick Brontë, living in the very midst of the Luddite risings—Cartwright's Mill was only three miles from Hartshead—was soon known as one of the Tory clergy of the neighbourhood, who fearlessly stood for the authority of the law when the local magistrates were afraid to interfere. It was in this year, 1812, that Mr. Brontë began to carry about with him a loaded pistol, for self-preservation in his long, solitary walks—a habit that was continued all his life. "It lay on his dressing-table with his watch," says Mrs. Gaskell; "with his watch it was put on in the morning; with his watch it was taken off at night." As Mr. Brontë lived to a good old age, and is not known to have killed any one, he must have been a careful man.

This, then, was the curate of Hartshead-cum-Clifton, who in the summer of 1812 met and fell in love with Miss Maria Branwell of Penzance.

She was twenty-nine—several years older than Mary Burder—"extremely small in person, not pretty, but very elegant." Her father, a much-respected merchant in Penzance, was dead ; but her home was in Penzance, and when she met Mr. Brontë she was on a visit to an uncle, Mr. Fennell, a clergyman who then kept a boys' school in the neighbourhood of Hartshead.

[1] Mrs. Gaskell's *Life of Charlotte Brontë*.

It was a very happy summer. "Cousin Jane" was already engaged to Mr. Morgan, another young curate; and there was at least one romantic picnic at Kirkstall Abbey, with Mr. Morgan and Mr. Brontë in admiring attendance. Maria Branwell was a demure little person, but she was not wanting in spirit. She was, in fact, remarkably well educated for her day, and, as her letters show, had quite a literary gift of her own. "For some years," she explained to her lover in one of her letters, "I have been perfectly my own mistress, subject to no control whatever"; and she makes her shy little boast that at home, in Penzance, she had always been the small pivot on which her family had habitually turned. And for this very reason, she assures him, she had often herself felt the need of a "guide and instructor." Charming, old-world letters are those of Maria Branwell to Patrick Brontë in the summer of 1812.[1] Long years after, when Charlotte Brontë had become famous as the author of *Jane Eyre*, her father put them into her hands, " telling me they were mamma's, and that I might read them." And she did read them, " in a frame of mind I cannot describe. . . . There is a rectitude," she wrote, " a refinement, a constancy, a modesty, a sense, a gentleness about them indescribable."

It cost Maria Branwell something, as may be seen in these little love-letters, to give up the home and the people she loved so much. But she does give them up; the prospect of being the companion of this brilliant Irishman's pilgrimage seems to her more delightful than anything this world can present. After a brief courtship, she and Cousin Jane are to be married on the same day; the wedding-cake is being made at home. Uncle Fennell, unlike Uncle Burder, gave his daughter and his niece away. The Rev. Mr. Morgan married Brontë to Maria, and then the Rev. Mr. Brontë " performed the same kind office " for Morgan and Cousin Jane.

Did the gentle little woman ever know that there had been another romance in an Essex village, where

[1] Mr. Clement Shorter's *Charlotte Brontë and her Circle*.

HAWORTH

the church had a green copper spire that glittered in the sun? Did she ever realise that she had caught her brilliant lover, the "Guide and Instructor," the "Beloved Friend," the "*Dear, Saucy Pat*" of those faded love-letters—on the rebound?

CHAPTER II

HAWORTH

MR. AND MRS. BRONTË remained at Hartshead for three years after their marriage, and from there they moved to Thornton, near Bradford, where the Morgans were already settled. The two eldest children, Maria and Elizabeth, were born at Hartshead, and the other four, Charlotte, Branwell, Emily, and Anne, at Thornton. Anne was a baby in 1820, when once more the little family was on the move—this time to the old stone parsonage at Haworth, that was afterwards to be so famous as the home of the Brontës.

Haworth may not have been exactly the parish of Patrick Brontë's dreams. In his stirring college days this ardent young Ulster Protestant, an excellent shot, and drilling shoulder to shoulder with the flower of British aristocracy, had perhaps conjured up his own fair vision of a Church militant; and Haworth was a straggling parish of hamlets, high up on the Yorkshire moors, four miles from Keighley and ten miles from Bradford; and in those days, when there were no railways and no motors, when there was not even a bicycle for a poor perpetual curate with a large family, Haworth must have seemed pretty well cut off from the world. The village was a single irregular street, bleak and stony, built on the side of a hill, with the moors stretching away behind it—a village "embedded in the moors." Its inhabitants were mostly woollen weavers, and of a very different type from the easy-going, rural population of Drumballyroney in County Down: strong-headed, independent, rough-spoken men and women these, who could hold their own with any parson that came among them. In fact, Haworth bade fair to be a stormy parish. The appointment was in the hands of the vicar of Bradford and trustees; and Mr. Brontë's immediate predecessor, Mr. Redhead, who had been appointed without the sanction of the trustees, had been very warmly received. For three successive Sundays there had been uproarious rioting in Haworth Church, till on his third, and last, appearance Mr. Redhead had been forced to escape from the pulpit to the Black Bull Inn, and thence, by the back-door, on horseback along the Keighley road, the turnpike gates being shut behind him to keep back an infuriated mob.

This was the pleasant parish to which Mr. Brontë— a good fighting parson, as we know—had been appointed; but this time vicar and trustees were agreed, and order had been miraculously restored in Haworth Church. "A lawless, yet not unkindly, population," Mrs. Gaskell calls them; and Mr. Brontë seems, from the time he came among them, to have commanded their respect, if he did not succeed in awaking their religious fervour.

The eighteenth-century church, once famous as the scene of Grimshaw's fanaticism and Wesley's eloquence, was now hard pressed by the Baptist and Methodist chapels grown up about it; and they were all more or less dominated by the Black Bull Inn in their midst. Drinking, cock-fighting, "arvills," and other rough, north-country practices still prevailed among the people of Haworth.

But Mr. Brontë was a man of forty-three, with six young children—five of them girls—and a delicate wife. If he had thought to add a little to his income by literature, he had been disappointed. His little literary ventures in poetry and prose—*The Rural Ministry; The Cottage in the Wood, or the Art of becoming Rich and Happy; The Maid of Killarney, or Albion and Flora*—had all fallen rather flat; they were probably all back on his hands as "remainders" before he accepted

HAWORTH

the living of Haworth. Mrs. Brontë, poor little woman, had done her best to encourage his literary efforts; she had even written something herself—a paper called "The Advantages of Poverty in Religious Concerns"—intended "for insertion in one of the periodical publications." But this was apparently never "placed"; and the neat little manuscript, carefully preserved among her husband's papers, came into Charlotte Brontë's hands with the faded packet of her mother's love-letters.

And so the living of Haworth was not to be despised. It offered security of tenure, a parsonage-house, and an income of nearly £200 a year; and, with his wife's annuity of £50, this was enough to live upon. One day in February 1820 seven heavily laden carts bearing the new parson's worldly goods lumbered through Haworth village towards the church and parsonage—the "long, low, oblong, stone parsonage," with its flagged roof, its garden, treeless and bleak, and its background of moors. The churchyard, full of upright gravestones, came ominously close up against two sides of the house.

Anne, the month-old baby, was christened soon after their arrival at Haworth. Mr. Morgan came from Bradford to officiate—probably accompanied by Cousin Jane. If so, Anne's christening was one of the last of those demure little clerical festivities—reminder of the picnic at Kirkstall Abbey and all the other pleasant incidents of their double courtship in the summer of 1812. For soon afterwards Mrs. Brontë was very ill, and her illness—an internal cancer—made it impossible for her to have the children much with her in the sickroom; and so it was that the little things were sent out, the seven-year-old Maria in charge, hand-in-hand on to the fresh, wild moors. And the parson tramped his parish, returning to his solitary meal, or to his wife's sick-room, and to the window from which he could watch for the little fledgling brood coming deviously homeward in the sunset. A woman from the village came to help their one little servant, Nancy Garrs, and Mr. Brontë "would allow nobody to take the night-nursing except himself."

"The companion of his pilgrimage," she had called herself! Perhaps their married life had not been altogether happy. Perhaps the quiet little woman, who had been "perfectly her own mistress," and "subject to no control whatever," had found her brilliant Irishman a difficult man to live with. For Patrick Brontë was a man of contradictions. He was a son of the soil, with the tastes and habits of a scholar, a self-made man, stoically independent, and a Tory to the backbone. He was a man of laudable ambitions, violent prejudices, and some rather petty foibles. Nature had not intended him for a parson; he was far more fitted to be a soldier, or a fighting politician. At forty-three he was beginning to feel that the world was not giving him the recognition he deserved; and, perhaps all the more because of this, he was a man who liked to be "master in his own house"—which usually means having his own way in little things.

But, such as he was, he was her brilliant Irishman, her lord and master, to the end. It is not fair to suppose that Maria Branwell ever regretted marrying Mr. Brontë. Many stories have been told of his tempestuous ways, his tyrannical temper—how, on one occasion, he burnt the children's shoes; how, on another, he cut up his wife's new gown. Most of these stories are allowed to have been the gossip of the kitchen and the village, and a good deal exaggerated in the telling; but, even so, how human they are after all! Those little domestic broils—who does not remember Mrs. Carlyle's anger and obstinacy when her poor mother filled the candlesticks with wax-candles on the occasion of some little Carlylean festivity? And who does not remember her lifelong remorse? Perhaps Mr. Brontë did lose his temper when the worthy Morgans, from the affluence of their Bradford living, sent those little shoes to the children, so much too smart for the children of a poor country clergyman to wear! And as for the story about Mrs. Brontë's buff print dress, which her husband cut up because he disliked "balloon" sleeves—does not that type of man always interfere about his wife's dress?

THE TRAGEDY OF COWAN BRIDGE

There was another devoted autocrat who insisted on accompanying his wife to her dressmaker's, and when he got there, waved his hand majestically and explained, "This lady wishes to be measured for a suit of clothes." By Nancy Garr's account, Mr. Brontë made his amends by trudging all the way to Keighley and bringing home under his arm a piece of silk for another, better gown. In those eight years during which she had accompanied his pilgrimage, his wife must have learnt that Patrick Brontë's pace was not quite suited to her own: she must have been well accustomed to his little ways. "Look, Nancy, what master has done!" she cried, carrying into the kitchen her buff print gown, from which the balloon sleeves had been so ruthlessly cut away. "Never mind; this falls to your share, Nancy."

And so to the last. "Ought I not to be thankful," she would say, "that he never gave me an angry word?" And perhaps, when she said it, she believed she was speaking the truth. Blessed are the meek. Towards the end of her life she liked to be raised up in bed to watch the nurse clean her bedroom grate, "because she did it as it was done in Cornwall."

CHAPTER III

THE TRAGEDY OF COWAN BRIDGE

EVERYBODY is agreed that the little Brontës were extraordinarily precocious children, and that after their mother's death they clung together in a wonderful fashion. Maria, at seven years old, was quite capable of mothering the other children. She was "grave, thoughtful, and quiet, to a degree far beyond her years." There was no nursery at the parsonage, but a little extra room upstairs had even then come to be known as "the children's study." Here little Maria would sit and read the newspaper, and afterwards ladle out to the others all sorts of information about politics, home and foreign, and the public characters of the day. The little Brontës—five girls and one boy—had few toys and no children's books, but they read the books in Mr. Brontë's study, and anything else that came in their way ; and they acted little plays of their own, taking for their characters their various heroes in politics and history. They would dispute as to the "comparative merits" of Wellington, Bonaparte, Hannibal, and Cæsar. When their arguments became too hot, the parson would stalk in among them as "arbitrator" ; and "in the management of these concerns" the widower would tell himself that his children were surely more precocious and cleverer than any children he had ever known before.

It was possibly the sight of Maria, at eight years old, reading the *Leeds Intelligencer*, with her little legs crossed, and the baby Anne "picking out the politicians of the day," that induced Mr. Brontë to write the letter—if, indeed, he ever did write that letter—to his old flame Mary Burder, at Wethersfield in Essex. For Mary Burder, who afterwards married Mr. Sibree, minister of the Wethersfield meeting-house, was still unmarried when Mrs. Brontë died in September 1821. The twelve years that had gone by since her flirtation with the Irish curate had passed lightly over Mary Burder's pretty head. She had had other suitors—among them Mr. Sibree. When she was quite an old lady, she told her daughter that, after Mrs. Brontë's death, Mr. Brontë wrote her a letter asking her if she would marry him and be the mother of his children. But Mary Burder had no mind to marry a widower with six little ones, and about a year after she received Mr. Brontë's letter she married Mr. Sibree.[1] It must have been about this time that Miss Elizabeth Branwell, Mrs. Brontë's elder sister, went to Haworth to take charge of Mr. Brontë's household and her dead sister's children.

Miss Branwell was a dignified little lady of the olden school, who had lived all her life at Penzance. Like her sister, she had her own little annuity of £50 a year.

[1] Mr. Augustine Birrell's *Charlotte Brontë*.

THE TRAGEDY OF COWAN BRIDGE 21

She was rather prim in manner, dressed always in silk gowns, with a large cap, and a " front " of light auburn curls on her forehead. She used a gold eyeglass attached to a long gold chain, and she took snuff out of a pretty little gold snuffbox, which she liked to hand to her friends, with a little laugh of enjoyment at their look of momentary discomfiture. She, too, was a great reader. On summer afternoons and in the long winter evenings she used to read aloud to her brother-in-law. At tea-time they would discuss what they had been reading, and on these occasions it was noticed that Miss Branwell " tilted argument without fear against Mr. Brontë." Poor little lady, she did her best. She missed the charms of Penzance society; in her time she had been one of its belles. At Haworth there was no society at all, from one year's end to the other. The moorland roads were rough, and the clergymen who occasionally came to the parsonage on clerical business did not bring the ladies of their family with them. The climate of the north did not suit Miss Branwell; she felt the parsonage cold and damp, and went clicking about the house on pattens, afraid of taking chills on the stone-flagged floors. In summer the heathery moors, so passionately loved by the Brontë children, were pleasant enough walking, even for a prim little maiden lady in a silk gown; but in winter, when storms swept over the moors and howled about the parsonage, Miss Branwell would shiver, and talk affectionately of Penzance.

About three years after his wife's death, Mr. Brontë decided on sending his daughters to Cowan Bridge School. It was an inexpensive school, recently started, for the daughters of poor clergymen, in a village on the coach-road between Leeds and Kendal—the Leeds and Kendal coach stopped at Keighley, which was only four miles from Haworth. The terms were manageable—only £14 a year for each child, with a small additional sum for books and clothing. The little girls wore a uniform dress and cloak, and plain straw cottage bonnets. As may be imagined, the school was not entirely self-supporting. An annual sum, to be raised by subscription, was to pay for the education, while the fees were to cover board and lodging. The treasurer, secretary, and originator of the whole scheme was the Rev. Carus Wilson of Casterton Hall, near Kirby Lonsdale. Such a school was greatly needed, and, almost before it was opened, many children's names had been put down for vacancies as they should occur. Little wonder that Mr. Brontë and his sister-in-law, poring together over the " Regulations " of a school that promised " a solid and sufficient English education," should think it the very place for the little girls who, unless they married curates, must all earn their own livelihood some day; and, clever as they were, the children had as yet learnt nothing " systematically."

And so in July 1824, the infant prodigies being just recovered from measles and whooping-cough, Mr. Brontë himself took the two eldest, Maria and Elizabeth, to Cowan Bridge, and a month or two later he went again, taking with him Charlotte and Emily.

Cowan Bridge must have been a pretty place in summer. The school was an enlarged cottage, long and bow-windowed, standing in its own garden, and the little hamlet on the roadside was built about a bridge over the Leck—a stream overgrown with alders, willows, and hazel-nuts. The school itself was run on economical lines, for in those first months of its existence the " subscriptions " were scarcely as yet forthcoming. The dietary looked, on paper, plentiful and wholesome enough. The breakfast of porridge, the supper of bread-and-milk, the joints, baked and boiled. the " potato pie " and plain, wholesome puddings— what could be better ? Mr. Carus Wilson ordered in the food, engaged the teachers and the servants, inspected the school, interviewed the cook—in fact, did all that a " mere man " could do to ensure that this school for little girls was properly managed. Alas ! the cook was dirty, careless, and extravagant; the house was damp, the dormitories were ill-ventilated. The church (where Mr. Carus Wilson himself preached) was

THE BRONTË CHILDREN AT HOME

more than two miles' walk from the school, and was unwarmed in winter. The children were afraid to complain to the teachers; the teachers were afraid to complain to Mr. Carus Wilson. It was hard enough discipline for robust children; for Maria Brontë, the little, delicate, old-fashioned girl who had mothered the other children ever since she was seven years old, it was positive martyrdom. In the eight months she spent at Cowan Bridge, Maria Brontë pined and drooped. Her cough became so bad that her little side was blistered, and she could scarcely drag herself out of her dormitory bed and dress herself in the cold winter mornings.

Early in 1825 an epidemic of low fever broke out in the school. The little Brontës did not have the fever, but Maria was anyhow so ill that the school authorities became frightened, and Mr. Brontë—who had known nothing of his child's condition—was suddenly sent for to take her home. Her school companions—her three little sisters among them—stood out on the roadside by the bridge over the Leck, an awestruck little band, to watch the Leeds coach carry the parson and his dying child away. Maria Brontë died at home on May 6th; a fortnight later, Elizabeth was sent home ill, and the very next day, June 1st, Mr. Brontë sent for, or fetched, the other two children, Charlotte and Emily. Elizabeth died on June 15th. Maria and Elizabeth died of what was in those days vaguely diagnosed as "rapid decline." They were both buried with their mother in Haworth Church.

CHAPTER IV

THE BRONTË CHILDREN AT HOME

ONCE more the Brontë children—the four that were left—found themselves together in the "children's study." Nancy Garrs had been succeeded by "Tabby," a woman belonging to Haworth village, who was to be an inmate of the parson's family for thirty years. Tabby was a strong character, a typical Yorkshire woman, and during her long and faithful service she came to be regarded as one of the Brontë family. She ruled in the parsonage kitchen, and looked after the children too, in her rough and kindly fashion. Aunt Branwell, as time went on, lived more and more in her own room upstairs, where she was surrounded by her little possessions—her "Indian work-box," her "japanned dressing-box," and the other souvenirs of her Cornish home. There Charlotte, Emily, and Anne came for their regular morning lessons. Miss Branwell was an accomplished needlewoman; hers were the days of the sampler and the fine muslin tuck. She mapped out methodically the children's "plan of the day"; and the girls grew up good needlewomen, and were all taught to take their share in the housework, especially the ironing and bread-baking that seem to have been always going on at the parsonage. The one boy— Branwell, as he was called in the family, though his name was Patrick Branwell—was his aunt's favourite; and from all accounts Branwell Brontë was a very clever and "taking" child, with the handsome face and the red head and the same ebullient, winning ways that his Irish father had before him. In fact, father, aunt, and sisters—everybody at Haworth parsonage—combined to adore Branwell Brontë. Their hopes were centred on him, the one boy among so many girls; while among the rough Haworth folk "t' vicar's Patrick" was trotted out for his cleverness and his wonderful and pretty ways, from the time when he was first big enough to run off and make friends for himself in Haworth village.

The parson was strongly advised to send his son to school; but his own boyhood was still fresh in his memory. For all his dignified bearing, with his chin wrapped in his voluminous clerical cravat, he had not forgotten those evenings, after his day's work at the hand-loom, spent among the books in Andrew Harshaw's little cottage study. He had been a village

THE BRONTË CHILDREN AT HOME

schoolmaster himself before he worked his way to Cambridge and was ordained a parson. Perhaps, too, he had had enough of "inexpensive schools for the children of poor clergymen." Anyhow, Mr. Brontë thought that, with a little assistance from the Haworth grammar school, he could educate his boy himself. He little knew what he was laying up for his old age!

Life at the parsonage was curiously uneventful. The parson breakfasted with his children, and the meal was conversational, if not hilarious. The breakfast itself was of the simplest—oatmeal porridge, of which the dogs had a generous share. The girls learnt their lessons in their aunt's room, the boy his in his father's study. The parson was punctual in the performance of his parochial duties; but he knew too much of the Yorkshire character to attempt to "mell" with his parishioners, and his sermons were extempore and always short. He had plenty of time for long, solitary tramps on the moors; and the moors were so wild in his day that he told Mrs. Gaskell he had seen "eagles stooping low in search of food for their young." Mr. Brontë always dined alone in his study, and Miss Branwell usually presided over the family dinner—another very simple meal, consisting always of a joint, baked or boiled, and a milk pudding. Tea-time at the parsonage was another conversational meal. It was a strongly political household, Tory and anti-Catholic, and there was never any lack of talk where Mr. Brontë was. "Papa" and Branwell used to walk to Keighley for the newspaper, the *Leeds Intelligencer*, "a most excellent Tory newspaper," and a family friend. But the parson took also the Whig *Leeds Mercury*, and they saw *John Bull*—described as "high Tory, very violent." *Blackwood's Magazine* was lent them by a neighbour, and the children had been taught to regard it with veneration as "the most able periodical there is." Sometimes, in this remote village, the parson's family was literally absorbed in politics. There were times when they could think and talk of nothing but "the great Catholic question"; the Duke of Wellington and

Mr. Peel; the culminating scene in the House of Lords, with the royal dukes in their robes; the "Great Duke," in green sash and waistcoat, standing up to read his speech, and all the peeresses fluttering up like doves. Aunt thought Mr. Peel's terms excellent—the Catholics "could do no harm with such good security"—and papa said the Duke of Wellington's words were "like precious gold."[1] Who shall say that little girls are not born politicians?

But at other times the Brontë children would gather, in the dusk of cold winter afternoons, round the kitchen fire—that dear old stone-flagged kitchen where Tabby reigned supreme, and little Anne was allowed to kneel upon a chair to watch the hot cakes lifted from the oven. Here, in the firelight—for Tabby was sparing of candles—they planned out their "Play of the Islanders." Each child chose an island, and peopled it with the great men of literature and history; and gradually "Tales of the Islanders" grew to be quite a lengthy work, filling four volumes, and becoming a part of their strange young lives; for by this time all four children were inveterate little scribblers in prose and verse. Their "Little Magazines" were written, booklet after booklet, in a handwriting so small that it cannot be read without the help of a magnifying glass. They included dramas, poems, and romances, as many as 35,000 words being written in eighteen pages—"an immense amount of manuscript," says Mrs. Gaskell, "in an incredibly small space."

It is perhaps worth while remembering here that those were the days of the Annuals. Popular literature was at rather a low ebb, and many devices were resorted to to make one Annual outshine another. The *Bijou Almanac* for 1837—dedicated to Queen Adelaide—was bound in gilt vellum, enclosed in a purple velvet case, and *sold with a magnifying glass;* so the Brontë children were only a year or two in advance of their time when they invented their "little writing," and filled their booklets with manuscript that cannot be de-

[1] Mrs. Gaskell's *Life of Charlotte Brontë.*

THE BRONTË CHILDREN AT HOME

ciphered by the naked eye. They had, however, no gilt vellum bindings. They wrote usually in little penny or twopenny books; but now and then the parson would bring them home a present of a sixpenny book, and inside the cover of this they would find inscribed, "*All that is written in this book must be in a good, plain, legible hand.—P. B.*"

They were all hero-worshippers, and their heroes for the most part were Toriest of the Tory. The Duke of Wellington was a kind of hereditary hero-in-chief. He permeated almost everything that Charlotte Brontë wrote; and not he only, but his sons—Lord Charles Albert Florian Wellesley and the Marquis of Douro—were always cropping up all through the "Little Magazines," as either heroes of romance, or as the imaginary authors of the manuscripts themselves; while their father, the Iron Duke, lounged at his ease in an armchair in Downing Street, "smoking a homely tobacco-pipe, for he disdained all the modern frippery of cigars." And it was so with their toys and games; the Duke was always of the company.

The parson had come home late one night from Leeds, bringing a box of soldiers for Branwell; and before breakfast the next morning each child had selected one particular soldier, named it, and surrounded it with romance. "This is the Duke of Wellington! This shall be the Duke!" cried Charlotte. She had chosen "the prettiest of the whole, and the tallest, and the most perfect in every part."

These children may have led very simple lives; they were only the children of a poor country clergyman—but who shall say that the childhood of the Brontës was unhappy?

CHAPTER V

MISS WOOLER'S SCHOOL

Miss Wooler's school, to which Charlotte Brontë was sent in January 1831, was one of those happy and well-managed "boarding-schools for young ladies" that really did exist in the days before the university education of women. "Roehead," as it was called, was a country house, standing in a large field, with lawn and trees about it, off the Leeds and Huddersfield highroad, about twenty miles from Haworth. Miss Wooler's pupils—some eight or nine girls—were most of them daughters of well-to-do families in the neighbourhood. Among them were Ellen Nussey of "the Rydings," Birstall, and Mary and Martha Taylor, whose family lived at the Red House, Gomersal. Miss Wooler, a plump, dignified little woman, has been described as in appearance "like a lady abbess." She wore well-fitting white embroidered gowns, exquisitely neat at throat and wrists, and her hair was plaited to form a coronet, from which long ringlets fell to her shoulders. She was a kind-hearted, sensible woman, and motherly to her girls, and she seems to have been a born teacher. On Saturday half-holidays she herself took her pupils for long walks. She knew her neighbourhood thoroughly, and many were the "true stories" she could tell the girls, as they trooped with her along the lanes, of the romantic old houses of the West Riding gentry, with their duels and their ghosts, and the not less romantic woollen factories—Cartwright's famous mill among them—rich in more recent memories. From Miss Wooler the girls heard all about the Luddite riots, the mill-workers' hatred of machinery, the secret nightly drilling of desperate men on those Yorkshire moors. Miss Wooler was a very benevolent person—life governor, in her time, of several charitable institutions, though

MISS WOOLER'S SCHOOL

her income was never a large one. Her personal sympathies were with Church and State, but the neighbourhood was strongly Nonconformist. At Roehead, the one or two pupils who were true-blue Tories and Churchwomen were more than held in check by the brilliant little red-hot Nonconformist Radicals. Among the former was Ellen Nussey of "the Rydings," while Mary and Martha Taylor, from Gomersal, were fiery little Radicals. "We used to be furious politicians," says Mary Taylor, writing of those school-days, "as one could hardly help being in 1832."[1]

It was to this school that Charlotte Brontë came on a cold day in January 1831, when Mary Taylor, watching from the window, first saw her future friend "coming out of a covered cart, in very old-fashioned clothes, and looking very cold and miserable."

"When she appeared in the schoolroom her dress was changed, but just as old. She looked a little old woman, so short-sighted that she always appeared to be seeking something, and moving her head from side to side to catch a sight of it. She was very shy and nervous, and spoke with a strong Irish accent. When a book was given her, she dropped her head over it till her nose nearly touched it; and when she was told to hold her head up, up went the book after it, still close to her nose, so that it was not possible to help laughing."[2]

But Ellen Nussey, the quiet, gentle-mannered English girl, stole up behind the little new-comer on that first day of her arrival among them, when she was "standing by the schoolroom window, looking out on the snowy landscape and crying, while all the rest were at play." Ellen Nussey, also, thought her an odd-looking little creature; but somehow the two girls were drawn together. There, in that bow-window, looking out on the snow, Ellen Nussey was "allowed to give sympathy." It was the beginning of a lifelong friendship.

Of course Charlotte Brontë was found to be "not well grounded." It was an awful moment when Miss Wooler proposed putting her into the junior class till

[1] Mrs. Gaskell's *Life*. [2] *Ibid*.

she could "overtake the girls of her own age." Charlotte Brontë cried so bitterly that the schoolmistress saw she had made a mistake, and put her into the first class, trusting to the girl's own ambition to push her into line with the others. And, if she were not "well grounded," Charlotte Brontë was able to teach her schoolfellows things hitherto undreamed of in Roehead philosophy. They found she already knew all the poetry they "had to learn by heart," and could give them short biographies of all the poets. She drew better than they did, and knew all about the great painters and their pictures. She "picked up every scrap of information concerning painting, sculpture, poetry, music, &c.," says Mary Taylor, "as if it were gold." She knew all about the "Ministries" of the day. She explained to the other girls that she had "taken an interest in politics since she was five years old." And of course she trotted out the Duke of Wellington, and shook her head over Sir Robert Peel; and, when they accused her of "always talking about clever people," such as Johnson and Sheridan, she fired up. She was a fiery little mortal when she liked. "Now, you don't know the meaning of *clever*. Sheridan might be clever; yes, Sheridan *was* clever—scamps often are; but Johnson hadn't a spark of *cleverality* in him." And the girls who had been "well grounded" knew that there was no such word as *cleverality*, and laughed; but they did not follow her distinction.

They left her out of their games of ball—she was too short-sighted and too puny. She used to stand about, or sit in some corner—always with a book under her nose—while they played together. But when they were tired of games, and wanted to listen to "a story," when they wanted to be carried away on the wings of romance—up on the rose-tipped clouds, or down into the dark, mysterious depths of things—then there was nobody like little Charlotte Brontë. So it had been with another, a greater novelist than she, whose infirmity kept him aloof while his companions played lustily in the yard of the old Edinburgh High School,

MISS WOOLER'S SCHOOL

but whose genius, like a magnet, drew them all about him, to listen, breathless, muddy, and open-mouthed, while he strung for them his wonderful romances—the little lame boy, who was to be "the author of *Waverley*," the Wizard of the North. There was nobody like Charlotte Brontë when the girls at Miss Wooler's school were in a mood for romance; for they had discovered that Charlotte Brontë could "make out." What a gift in a girls' boarding-school!

"*Make it out!*" cried Mary Taylor eagerly—even Radicals like a little romance now and then—"*Make it out! I know you can!*"

At night, in the dormitory, the girls would gather about her in the dark, trembling with excitement; and so powerful was the effect on her dimity-curtained audience that once, at least, poor Miss Wooler, enjoying a quiet hour after the fatigues of the day, was alarmed by a "piercing scream," and hurried upstairs to find that "Charlotte Brontë had been telling them a story," and that one of her enthralled listeners had been "seized with violent palpitations."

And so the odd-looking, painstaking little girl did "overtake" her companions—nay, she became a small authority amongst them; and so curiously popular was she that on one occasion, when Miss Wooler gave her a bad mark for not knowing her lesson in Blair's *Belles Lettres*, the other pupils—instigated, of course, by the little arch-militant Mary Taylor—actually rebelled on her behalf, and organised a strike. It was unjust to punish Charlotte Brontë, the most studious and dutiful among them. Arbitration failed, and the girls could only be induced to return to work by the unqualified withdrawal of that bad mark.

Thus a year and a half passed, and the day came for Charlotte Brontë to leave Roehead. She had made good progress in French and drawing, and no doubt she had been "well grounded" in everything else. Ellen Nussey's school-days, and Mary and Martha Taylor's also, were coming to a close. The friends were to be separated, to meet again now and then, and to correspond affectionately with each other. Ellen Nussey and Charlotte Brontë were to remain firm friends till death parted them. Ellen Nussey was to keep all her friend's letters—about five hundred—without which no biographer could have understood Charlotte Brontë's character, and no real biography of her could ever have been written. Miss Wooler did not lose sight of her pupils: the day was to come when Charlotte Brontë returned to Roehead as one of Miss Wooler's assistant-teachers. But in the early summer of 1832 there was no thought of this.

CHAPTER VI

THE PRIDE OF THE FAMILY

THE chief event at the parsonage, on Charlotte Brontë's home-coming, seems to have been that Aunt Branwell had consented to take in *Fraser's Magazine*. Otherwise, the little family were going on much as usual. The parson was not quite so strong as he used to be; the aunt was, as usual, indulging in "pleasant reminiscences about the salubrious climate of Penzance." Charlotte, now that she had been "well grounded," was to "instruct" Emily and Anne; and Mr. Brontë had arranged for a teacher of drawing—one William Robinson, of Leeds, who had been for a somewhat indefinite period a pupil of Sir Thomas Lawrence—to come and give drawing lessons at the parsonage. Charlotte Brontë writes to Ellen Nussey—already her "*dear, dear, dear* Ellen":—

"An account of one day is an account of all. In the morning, from nine o'clock till half-past twelve, I instruct my sisters and draw; then we walk till dinner-time. After dinner, I sew till tea-time, and after tea I either write, read, or do a little fancy-work, or draw, as I please. Thus, in one delightful, though somewhat monotonous, course my life is passed. I have been out only twice to tea since I came home. We are expecting company

THE PRIDE OF THE FAMILY

this afternoon, and on Tuesday next we shall have all the female teachers of the Sunday-school to tea."

Evidently the parson and Aunt Branwell were doing their best to provide the young people with a little "social thrill." But the girls were intensely shy and reserved. As " t' vicar's daughters " they taught regularly in the Sunday-school, and a certain amount of visiting fell to their share. But they did not care to knock uninvited at cottage doors; and it was perhaps as well that tea-parties were few and far between, for "company," as they knew it at Haworth, had few charms for them. They had a positive aversion to strangers; in fact, to quote Mrs. Gaskell's phrase, the Miss Brontës "never faced their kind voluntarily." Charlotte, shy and retiring as she was, had a good deal of spirit. She could be combative on occasion; and, perhaps because she was the eldest, and had been at school, she talked better than the others. Anne, the youngest, was still a queer-looking, timid little thing, promising to be rather pretty; and Emily, with her lank figure and fine eyes, and her passionate love of all dumb creatures, was the least sociable and most persistently taciturn of the three. Mr. Birrell says of Emily Brontë that " her most obvious gift was silence."

But, whatever they were in " company," they found plenty to talk about when they were together. Never were sisters so attached. All their lives they were to be company enough for each other; and so, in their daily walks, they avoided Haworth village, with the opportunities it afforded of " facing their kind," and turned instead towards the fresh, wild moors—their beloved, breezy moors, the nursery of their childhood.

But they had something else to face. No bigger than a man's hand as yet, but already visible on the horizon, must have been the cloud that was to gather over the Brontë household, and to darken all their lives. " When it has been once written," says Mr. Birrell, " that the Brontës had a brother who was their dream, their delusion, their despair, the rest may be forgotten, or, better still, never known." But Branwell Brontë cannot be forgotten: he played too important a part in the family story for that. A great deal has been written about him, from the time of Charlotte Brontë's death, when the literary world was mourning her as a little russet martyr, down to the uncensorious present day, when men and women are finding too much good in everything. He has been handled too severely, and he has been handled too leniently, for, after all, he is not the first black sheep of a fold, nor the only son of the manse who has taken to evil courses. It is not a very unusual thing to find the boy of a family weaker, morally and mentally, than its daughters. Has nobody ever heard a careworn parent say with a sigh, pointing to a stalwart little girl with a cropped head and far-apart eyes, "*She ought to have been the boy*"? It was so with the Brontë family: the girls—though none of the Brontës were to be called stalwart—were all of stronger mettle than the boy. If it had not been for the place that, in spite of all their handicaps, they made for themselves in our literary history, nobody would have taken any notice of this particular boy's peccadilloes, except the employers who, one after another, were obliged to dismiss him, and the unhappy father and sisters who as often were obliged to take him back under the parsonage roof. He must be classed among the decadents—those creatures on the borderland who, as they develop, or fail to develop, show themselves unstable, unmoral, but who cannot be called insane. The characters of the sisters, who loved Branwell Brontë and bore with him and suffered for him, and especially the indomitable character and genius of little Charlotte Brontë, the eldest—a year older than he—have deflected literary interest on the son of this family. It is as their brother, as a factor in the story of their lives, that the unhappy boy must be remembered—for better, for worse.

If he had had brothers, it has been often asked; if he had been "licked into shape" at a public school; if he had emigrated, or enlisted, or run away to sea, or done anything except grow up at Haworth parsonage,

THE PRIDE OF THE FAMILY

where the parson, and Aunt Branwell, and his sisters, and everybody in Haworth village thought he was going to be a genius, would it have been otherwise with Branwell Brontë ? For it must be demoralising not to be a genius and to be thought one—far more demoralising than to be a genius and not to be thought one. Branwell Brontë was not a genius, and he was certainly not a manly boy. In his weak, exuberant way he pictured to himself a literary career such as a genius might make for himself, and he wrote a good deal—chiefly verse—after he had outgrown the period of those " Little Magazines," in which Charlotte and he were the chief contributors ; but there was no spark of real genius in his writings, and much of it is morbid, foolish, and hypocritical. He pictured for himself also the career of a great painter, and he talked about art and the Royal Academy, and he took lessons with Mr. Robinson, and painted portraits that are said to have " caught the likeness," but which otherwise were mere daubs. He pursued dreams and bucked at realities ; and the parson and Aunt Branwell and his sisters dreamed with him and for him, and tried one thing after another, doing their very utmost; for, whatever their mistakes, they loved the boy. All their hopes were set upon him ; he was the pride of the family.

" Sad as remembered kisses after death " is the story of this little red-headed idol of Haworth parsonage. Charlotte Brontë could dimly recall the picture of her mother playing with little Branwell in the evening dusk in the parlour at the parsonage. He must have been three years old then. And he must have been about ten years old when Aunt Branwell gave the children the three volumes of Scott's *Tales of a Grandfather*, recently published, with the little inscription in her own handwriting: "These volumes were written by Sir Walter Scott, and the Hugh Little John mentioned in them is Master Lockhart, grandson to Sir Walter. . . . A New Year's gift by Miss E. B. to her dear little nephew and nieces, Patrick, Charlotte, Emily, and Anne Brontë, 1828."[1]

[1] Mrs. Gaskell's *Life*.

He could not have been much older when Mr. Brontë came home from Leeds late at night with that box of wooden soldiers for Branwell in his pocket, and Branwell ran across to his sisters' door, before breakfast, to share the toy with them. And he was fifteen when the parson sent him as his sister Charlotte's "escort" on her first visit to Ellen Nussey at "the Rydings." It was a long drive, and the boy and girl drove together in the two-wheeled gig—the only vehicle to be had in Haworth except the "covered cart" that took Charlotte to Roehead. The boy was in a "wild ecstasy with everything." He walked about "in unrestrained boyish enjoyment," making sketches of the turret-roofed house, the rookery behind it, and the old chestnuts on the lawn. "He told his sister he was leaving her in Paradise, and if she were not intensely happy, she never would be."[1]

He was not without boy friends in Haworth, and with one of them especially he used often to go for long rambles on the moors. With him, about this time, he spent a day at Keighley Fair. It was the annual "feast" at Keighley, with the usual gingerbread stalls and spangled shows, the "Pandean pipes" and merry-go-rounds, and all the rest.

"As the evening advanced, and the shows were lighted up, Branwell's excitement, hilarity, and extravagance knew no bounds: he would see everything and try everything. Into a rocking-boat he and his friend gaily stepped. The rise of the boat when it reached its full height gave Branwell a pleasant view of the fair beneath; but, when it descended, he screamed out at the top of his voice, 'Oh, my nerves! my nerves! Oh, my nerves!' On each descent, every nerve thrilled, tingled, and vibrated . . ."[2]

And as the boys walked home that night along the Keighley road, Branwell, still excited, insisted on a wrestling match with his companion, and was promptly overthrown.

One more glimpse of a boy of twenty, when Mary

[1] Leyland's *The Brontë Family*.   [2] *Ibid.*

PEN, PALETTE, AND POET LAUREATE

and Martha Taylor are staying at the parsonage. Martha had kept up a " continual flow of good-humour " during her stay, and had " consequently been very fascinating."

" They are making such a noise about me," writes Charlotte to Ellen Nussey, " I cannot write any more. . . . Mary is playing on the piano, Martha is chattering as fast as her little tongue can run, and Branwell is standing before her, laughing at her vivacity." [1]

But this is anticipating, for this was in the summer of 1838, and by this time Charlotte Brontë must have been getting vaguely anxious about him. Branwell, though the family at the parsonage did not know it, was already on the downward path.

CHAPTER VII

THE PEN, THE PALETTE, AND THE POET LAUREATE

FOR a year or two after Charlotte Brontë left Miss Wooler's school, the sisters and brother lived happily enough under the parsonage roof. Charlotte told Mary Taylor, about this time, that she had been reading Cobbett. *She did not like him; but all was fish that came to her net.* One of the most remarkable things about this remarkable family is the amount of reading they got through, and the number of books they got hold of, on their very modest income, in a remote moorland village, before the days of cheap literature and cheap postage, and when public libraries were still undreamed of. Shakespeare, Milton, Pope, Goldsmith, Scott, Byron, Wordsworth, Southey—it would astonish a modern schoolgirl to learn what large and heavy fish came into Charlotte Brontë's net. Politics were part of the daily fare, but in the days following the passing of the Reform Bill politics were served up hot with every meal at the parsonage.

Mary Taylor and Charlotte Brontë were always at

[1] Mrs. Gaskell's *Life*.

daggers drawn about their politics and creeds. The Red House at Gomersal was a centre of "violent dissent and Radicalism." Mr. Taylor had brought up his sons and daughters "on republican principles," and from the Taylors Charlotte heard plenty of hard things about a "mercenary priesthood" and "a despotic aristocracy." She listened without saying much; she would even sometimes allow that there was "a *little* truth" in what they said. But she never budged from her own position. No doubt in her heart of hearts she was hugging the childish memory of that tall wooden soldier, "the most perfect in every part," that had always been her embodiment of all the virtues of the Great Duke, and all the political principles of the party to which he belonged. This it is to be a hero-worshipper!

In the intervals of literature and politics, the drawing lessons at the parsonage were great events. Branwell showed a talent for drawing, and said he would like to be a painter; so the parson did his best in providing the drawing-master from Leeds, at a charge of "two guineas a visit." Charlotte, in spite of her short-sightedness, was so fond of drawing that at first she too thought she might make a living by it, and she nearly ruined her eyesight by making minute and laborious copies of line-engravings, after the fashion of that day. Branwell, under Mr. Robinson's guidance, seems to have progressed so far as to paint, very badly, in oils. He painted an elaborate group-portrait of his sisters, and the painting, poor as it was, hung for years on the staircase at Haworth parsonage, opposite to the door of the "children's study." The family thought that Branwell wanted only opportunity to make a great painter; and the question was, could they afford to send him to London, as a pupil of the Royal Academy? Some of Mr. Robinson's friends were plying their art in the Great Babylon, and a good deal of talk about the Elgin Marbles, and Chantrey, and Haydon had filtered through to Haworth parsonage during those lessons of the drawing-master, at a charge of two guineas a visit. Branwell, at eighteen, rather liked the idea of going to

PEN, PALETTE, AND POET LAUREATE

London, and went so far as to write a letter to the secretary of the Royal Academy, asking for information. He had long dreamed of the Metropolis. He possessed a map of London, which he had studied till he seemed to know its very byways. He would astonish the London " bagmen " who put up at the " Black Bull " by knowing more about the " short-cuts " across London than they did. This, and the rather ominous faculty he had of writing with both hands at once—he is said to have been able to write two separate letters at the same time—earned for him a pleasant notoriety in Haworth circles. The landlord of the Black Bull rather counted upon " t' vicar's Patrick " to amuse his guests, and on these occasions the boy was " treated " rather more potently than was good for him. And so, in 1835, Charlotte writes to her friend Ellen, " We are all about to divide, break up, separate." Branwell was to go to London, Charlotte had been offered the post of teacher in Miss Wooler's school, and Emily was to go with her as a pupil.

L'homme propose. Emily stayed only three months at Miss Wooler's school; it was found that she could not live away from Haworth and the moorland air. After three months of school routine, Emily was so ill that Charlotte grew frightened, remembering the fate of Maria and Elizabeth. " Papa " was written to; Emily was despatched home, and Anne came as pupil in her place. The gentle Anne made out her two years at Roehead, and Charlotte remained there as teacher, with a salary, till early in 1838. It was not on the whole an unhappy time. Charlotte's friends, the Nusseys and the Taylors, lived in the neighbourhood, and Miss Wooler was exceedingly kind. However hard the day's work, Charlotte looked forward to her evenings when she and Miss Wooler sat together chatting, " sometimes late into the night." But she did not like " governessing " ; it was " nothing but teach, teach, teach from morning till night." And Charlotte confessed to Mary Taylor that, after she had clothed herself and Anne, nothing was left of her salary. She grew tired, depressed, overwrought; she was troubled by religious scruples; and her letters to Ellen Nussey reflect her moods.

The parson's expenses at this time were evidently a little beyond his means, and poor Emily had plucked up her courage and left home again to earn some money. She took a situation as teacher in a school near Halifax, where the duties were "hard labour from six in the morning till eleven at night"; and meantime Miss Wooler—to make matters worse for Charlotte and Anne—had, early in 1837, removed her school to Dewsbury Moor, not nearly so bracing a locality as Roehead.

The whole family had met under the parsonage roof for the Christmas holidays of 1836, and it was during those holidays that the famous letters were written—the letter from Charlotte to the poet Southey, and the letter from Branwell to the poet Wordsworth. These young people were nothing if they were not ambitious!

In the evenings the girls sat over the fire in the parlour. The parson read prayers at eight o'clock. Miss Branwell retired very early, and so did "Tabby," and Mr. Brontë, who spent the evenings in his own study, always went upstairs to bed punctually at nine. Every night, on the way to bed, he wound up the grandfather's clock that stood half-way up the staircase; and every night, as he passed the sitting-room door, he called out, "in stentorian tones," his little paternal formula, "*Don't be up late, children!*" And every night, just about this time, the girls folded and put away their sewing, and began to walk up and down the room. In the firelight—the candles put out—they walked and talked till late into the night—talked over their troubles, past and present, and over their future plans. It was during these Christmas holidays that they first talked of literature as a means of livelihood. They were all inveterate little "makers out." They had written prose, and they had written verse. But how to know what was the literary value of it all—whether there were any chance for it, and for them, in the great literary market? And so one day during these Christmas holidays, Charlotte Brontë plucked up courage to write a letter, enclosing some specimens of her verses, to Southey, the Poet Laureate. The sisters waited anxiously; but the Christmas holidays came to an end, and Charlotte and Anne returned to Miss Wooler's school, and Emily went back to Miss Patchett's school, and no answer had come from the Poet Laureate.

Nobody knows exactly what Branwell Brontë did in London, or why he came home again so very soon. Two things he certainly did—he saw Westminster Abbey (whether inside as well as outside is a matter of speculation), and he visited the Castle Tavern, Holborn, kept by the "veteran prize-fighter, Tom Spring," and "frequented by the principal sporting characters of the time."[1] There the boy's brilliant talk attracted some notice; and when the company became rather noisy in dispute over the dates of certain great battles, they asked him to be umpire. It was his one little social triumph, the last of his London dream; and to the bitter disappointment of his family—borne by them, however, with "Christian resignation"—Branwell Brontë returned to the parsonage, and to the lesser charms of the Black Bull Inn.

To do it justice, Haworth village seems to have welcomed the return of the prodigal. The landlord of the Black Bull and John Brown, the sexton, listened open-eyed to the young gentleman's account of Tom Spring; and perhaps the parson heard about the visit to Westminster Abbey. His Haworth friends persuaded Branwell to become a freemason, and he was proposed as a brother of the new Haworth lodge, the "Lodge of the Three Graces," of which John Brown, the sexton, was to be "worshipful master." And he was also elected—but perhaps this was the parson's proviso—secretary of the Haworth Temperance Society. The parson allowed him some more drawing lessons with Mr. Robinson; and while Emily was at Miss Patchett's school, Branwell was for a few months usher in another school near Halifax; and after that he took lodgings in Bradford, where Mr. Morgan—who had married

[1] Leyland.

"Cousin Jane"—did his best to find him employment as a portrait-painter. He painted portraits of Mr. Morgan, and of the vicar of Bradford, and also of his landlady and her children. This last commission seems to have been undertaken as part-payment of his landlady's bill—or, at least, his landlady thought so, for she made a great fuss when he left Bradford without having finished the portrait; and it is said that Mr. Thompson, who was also a portrait-painter in Bradford, kindly "put the finishing touches" to some of Branwell Brontë's unfinished work. But it was evident by this time—even to his own family—that Branwell Brontë was not going to be a great painter.

And apparently Charlotte was not to be a poet either. She had given up all hopes of hearing from Southey, when, in March 1837, his letter came. He had been away, and since his return had been struggling with arrears of correspondence; and he had left her letter to the very last, because it was a difficult one to answer. He did not like to "cast a damp over the high spirits and the generous desires of youth." He recognises her sincerity, though he suspects that the signature, "C. Brontë," is fictitious. She has asked for his opinion; but "the opinion may be worth little and the advice much." And he proceeds to offer it.

Southey's letter is long and carefully written. He admits that she possesses what Wordsworth called "the faculty of verse"; but so many people possess it also that he warns her of disappointment if she hopes to achieve distinction. Though he has never regretted having taken to it himself, he considers it his duty to warn all young men against literature as a perilous profession. As for women, "Literature," he says, "cannot be the business of a woman's life, and it ought not to be. The more she is engaged in her proper duties, the less leisure will she have for it, even as an accomplishment and a recreation." And then there follows an assurance that she is not to "disparage" her gift, but to "write poetry for its own sake."[1]

[1] Mrs. Gaskell's *Life*.

Charlotte's answer to Southey is too long to quote; but it should be read, for it is honest, modest, and brave. She accepts his advice gratefully, though it hurts her. She is not altogether the "idle, dreaming being" he seems to think her. She explains to him that she is the daughter of a poor clergyman, the eldest of the family, and a governess; that all day long her head and hands too are busy, and that though in the evenings she does think, she never troubles anybody with her thoughts. "I have endeavoured not only attentively to observe all the duties a woman ought to fulfil, but to feel deeply interested in them. I don't always succeed, for sometimes when I'm teaching or sewing I would rather be reading or writing; but I try to deny myself, and my father's approbation amply rewarded me for the privation." She trusts she shall never again feel ambitious to see her name in print; but "if the wish should rise, I'll look at Southey's letter, and suppress it."

Southey wrote again—a kind little note—asking her, if ever she is at the Lakes, to "let me see you." He adds a word of caution: "Take care of over-excitement, and endeavour to keep a quiet mind," and the correspondence ends with a " God bless you ! "

Poor Charlotte Brontë ! Long years after, she said to Mrs. Gaskell, "Mr. Southey's letter was kind and admirable, a little stringent, but it did me good." She had said practically the same thing to the contrite Mary Taylor, who once told her, when they were at school together, that she was "very ugly." "You did me a great deal of good, Polly, so don't repent of it."

The brave little woman was never to see Southey at the Lakes. When she was a celebrated novelist—after Southey was dead—and she and Mrs. Gaskell were staying at the Lakes with the Kaye-Shuttleworths, she told Mrs. Gaskell of his invitation. "But there was no money to spare," she explained, "nor any prospect of my ever earning money enough to have the chance of so great a pleasure, so I gave up thinking of it."

She had folded away her literary dreams with her

letters from the Laureate, and she set before herself the stern realities of life. "*Literature cannot be the business of a woman's life, and it ought not to be.*" She went on teaching at Miss Wooler's school, till her health broke down ; and when, in 1838, Miss Wooler insisted on her seeing a doctor, he ordered her, "as she valued her life," to go home at once.

Branwell, meantime, not to be behind his sister, had written to Wordsworth. He enclosed some verses, " the prefatory scene," as he explained, " to a much longer subject." It was not a pleasant poem ; it was the kind of excursion that Wordsworth himself would not voluntarily have undertaken. It endeavoured to " develop strong passions and weak principles struggling with a high imagination and acute feelings till, as youth hardens towards age, evil deeds and short enjoyments end in mental misery and bodily ruin." The " prefatory scene," however, did not go beyond the innocent infancy of the unhappy traveller into these lurid vistas, about whom Wordsworth was asked to believe that

" . . . often has my mother said,
While on her lap I laid my head,
She feared for Time I was not made
But for Eternity."

Wordsworth may not have recognised the "faculty of verse " or the ring of sincerity in Branwell's work that Southey found in Charlotte's. It is possible he looked rather glum over part of Branwell's letter. " Surely in this day," the young man had rashly written, " when there is not a *writing* poet worth a sixpence, the field must be open, if a better man can step forward."

It is not known what answer Wordsworth sent to Branwell Brontë; but he kept the poem and the letter, and after the Brontës had become famous, he gave them to his son-in-law, Edward Quilinan.

CHAPTER VIII

" QUALIFIED TO TEACH "

IT is rather pathetic to see how anxiously the parson cultivated the friendships his daughter Charlotte had made at school. In the summer of 1838, when Charlotte was two-and-twenty, she was sent home from Miss Wooler's school " a wreck." But as soon as the moorland air and " utter quiet " of home had revived her, Mr. Brontë arranged for Mary and Martha Taylor to come and stay at the parsonage. It was during this visit that Martha—Little Miss Boisterous, as she was called at school—made herself so fascinating. Charlotte always said that the society of the Taylor family was " one of the most rousing pleasures " she knew; and, indeed, their go-ahead Radicalism could not have been altogether in accord with the parsonage life. Once, at school, Mary told Charlotte that she and her family at the parsonage were " like potatoes, growing in the dark," and Charlotte had assented sadly, " Yes, I know we are." But Miss Branwell—who had moved in the best society in Penzance—had her reservations about the Misses Taylor. She did not approve of that freedom of speech that comes from being educated on republican principles, and on one occasion she felt it incumbent on her to correct Mary and Martha for their too liberal use of the verb " to spit." On the other hand, the gentle-mannered Ellen Nussey was admired by everybody at the parsonage. She came and went, in her placid way, upsetting nobody's feelings, and taking all the little eccentricities of the family for granted—the " calm, steady girl, not brilliant, but good and true."

It is to Ellen we owe the glimpses of Haworth parsonage at its best, of the parson, cravatted up to the chin, with his little whims and oddities, and his old-fashioned courtesy to a guest. It is Ellen who has described Aunt Branwell, in silk gown and mob-cap, dispensing the favours of her little gold snuffbox, reading aloud to the parson, and at tea-time "tilting argument without fear against Mr. Brontë." It was Ellen who wandered with the sisters on their beloved moors, who paced with them up and down the dining-room at night, after Mr. Brontë had wound up the clock and gone to bed, and all the parsonage was asleep. And when the girls sat together on the hearthrug in the firelight, even the dogs took possession of Ellen. Keeper, the bulldog, clambered awkwardly on to Emily's lap, and, finding it too small, stretched out his big body till it rested on Ellen's knees. Emily and Anne had "never seen anybody they liked so well." It is recorded of Ellen's first visit to the parsonage that the inscrutable Emily actually invited her to go for a walk; and Charlotte, waiting anxiously for their return, waylaid her friend at the front-door to whisper, "*How did she behave?*"—for Emily had never been known to do such a thing before. In after visits, Emily constituted herself a sort of silent bodyguard to Ellen Nussey, and it was in that capacity she warded off the attentions of the curate during an evening walk. Emily's nickname in the family, "the Major," dated from this incident. Shy and silent as Emily was, Ellen found her "intensely lovable." Her look and smile spoke more than words. One of those "rare, expressive looks" from the wonderful eyes of this enigmatic girl was to Ellen Nussey "something to remember through life."[1]

It was not till 1839 that the curates appeared on the Haworth horizon. When Mr. Brontë was well over sixty, and had been nearly twenty years at Haworth, his bishop allowed him the assistance of a curate, the Church Pastoral Aid Society supplying the necessary funds. The advent of this young man was not only a help to the parson, but it brought to the village and the parsonage just that "social thrill" of which they had hitherto been so much in need. For Mr. William

[1] Mr. Clement Shorter's *Charlotte Brontë and her Circle.*

"QUALIFIED TO TEACH"

Weightman was handsome, cheery, and good-tempered; and no sooner was he settled in his lodgings in the village than he found himself on more or less friendly terms with all the other curates in all the other parishes round about. They were all militant young Churchmen, in a veritable hotbed of dissent, and " the fighting gentry "—or " the Holyes," as Charlotte irreverently dubbed them—soon wakened up the neighbourhood with sermons on dissent, lectures at the Mechanics' Institute in Keighley, and a lively discussion about the payment of the Church rates. " Papa," who had hitherto lived on the most amicable terms with the Baptists and Methodists round about him, was put into the chair at a meeting in the schoolroom, supported by a curate on either side of him, and " Papa " was also made to deliver a lecture at the Mechanics' Institute, which was highly praised in the newspapers. Not only so : the fighting gentry came down on the parsonage. They came for tea and toast and theology, and they tilted High Church argument till even Charlotte, who thought them bigoted and intolerable, waxed eloquent behind the teapot. And they waylaid the young ladies in their hitherto solitary walks on the moors ; and when Mr. Weightman discovered that not one of the three Miss Brontës had ever received a valentine, he walked off to Keighley and posted—with an enviable impartiality—three of the prettiest and most romantic valentines he could select ; so that each young lady might feel she had seen the folly at least of one. Mr. Weightman had a pretty turn for pen-and-ink sketching. Charlotte was obliged to own that he possessed " something of the artist's eye." He wrote poetry, and he was a generous soul withal. When he was on holiday he did not forget his friends. " A prodigious quantity of game "—wild-ducks, grouse, partridges, snipes, curlews, and even a large salmon— arrived at the parsonage during Mr. Weightman's holidays. But alas ! the curate was as fickle as he was good-natured. It was impossible to tell with whom he was in love. At one time Miss Nussey appeared to be the object of his affections; at another, it was the gentle Anne. He sat opposite to Anne in church, and "sighed softly," looking at her "out of the corners of his eyes." It was certainly Anne. And then—it was another young lady altogether, of whom he came and talked to Charlotte; and Charlotte owned herself baffled. She began to think that Mr. Weightman was not really in love with anybody at all.

But by this time Charlotte Brontë had a lover of her own. The Rev. Henry Nussey—Ellen's brother—had met her at the Rydings. In 1839, when she was three-and-twenty, he was "comfortably settled" in a curacy at Donnington, in Sussex, and was "intending to take pupils." He wrote her a letter, explaining that in these circumstances he should want a wife to take care of the pupils, and he asked her to be that wife. In spite of a "kindly leaning" towards this unexceptionable young Churchman, Charlotte Brontë refused Henry Nussey, and so closed for herself this little chapter of somewhat prosaic romance. "Ten to one I shall never have the chance again; but *n'importe*."

They were not suited to each other. Something of Charlotte's Irish heritage cries out in her words to the faithful Ellen: "Why, it would startle him to see me in my natural home character; he would think I was a wild, romantic enthusiast indeed. I could not sit all day long making a grave face before my husband. I would laugh, and satirise, and say whatever came into my head first."

And then, in the next sentence, the gentle little dead mother seems to speak, more softly: "And if he were a clever man, and loved me, the whole world, weighed in the balance against his smallest wish, should be light as air."

Charlotte was right, and Henry Nussey saw it; and six months later he became engaged to somebody else. Nor very long afterwards Charlotte was to receive, and refuse, another offer of marriage—an offer of a more romantic nature. Mr. Bryce, a young Irish curate in the neighbourhood, "witty, lively, ardent, and clever

"QUALIFIED TO TEACH" 49

too," had accompanied his vicar on a visit to the parsonage. He "tilted argument" with Charlotte during the whole of one long happy afternoon, and a day or two afterwards he sent her "an ardent declaration and a proposal of matrimony." "Well," writes Charlotte to Ellen Nussey, "I have heard of love at first sight, but this beats all!"

Not even curates could banish from Haworth parsonage the stern realities of life. Charlotte had no inclination to marry Mr. Bryce, and, this being so, she must earn her own living, and earn it in the only way that seemed open to her—by "governessing." And so she turned to business with a "Let me have no more of your humbug about Cupid."[1]

Meanwhile, it could only have been during the holidays that Anne enjoyed the privilege of sitting with downcast eyes in the family pew. Early in 1839, not long after she left school, she went as governess to the children of Mrs. Ingham, at Blake Hall, Mirfield, not far from Roehead. At nineteen, Anne Brontë was still so shy and timid that Charlotte was afraid Mrs. Ingham would fancy she had "a natural impediment in her speech." But the girl insisted on going by herself to Mirfield, saying she could manage better if she were "thrown entirely on her own resources." She was not so unhappy with the Inghams, and stayed with them for some time. The gentlest and least intellectual of the sisters, she seems on the whole to have been the most successful as a governess.

Charlotte, in the same year, took a temporary situation with another Yorkshire family—the Sidgwicks, at Stonegappe—and there she seems to have been very unhappy indeed. The tradition in the Sidgwick family is that Charlotte Brontë was "in a very morbid condition the whole time." One of the sons remembers having thrown a Bible at her, and another of the family remembers that if she were asked to walk with them to church, she thought she was being "ordered about like a slave," and if she were not asked, she

[1] Mr. Clement Shorter's *Charlotte Brontë and her Circle*.

imagined she was being "excluded from the family circle." Her own letters to Emily at home—"Mine dear Love," and "Mine bonny Love," as she calls her —give the other side of the picture—a dreary picture indeed.

One does not like to think of little Charlotte Brontë— even now that she has been dead for more than half a century—"excluded from the family circle"; walking "a little behind" the master of the house, when he strolled through his fields with his children and his Newfoundland dog; sitting in the schoolroom, after the children were asleep in bed, making muslin night-caps and dressing dolls. One does not like to think that she was ever "taken to task" by any woman happier than herself for looking "depressed." And yet, it had to be. Southey would have thought it all right. She was only attaining "that degree of self-government" which Southey had recommended as "essential to our own happiness, and contributing greatly to that of those around us." *Literature could not be, and ought not to be, the business of a woman's life.* Even as late as 1855, when Mrs. Gaskell, herself a brilliant and successful authoress, was writing her *Life of Charlotte Brontë*, she could say: "Teaching seemed to her at this time, *as it does to most women at all times*, the only way of earning an independent livelihood." So much for the days that are no more!

On Charlotte's return home, "Tabby" was ill. Charlotte undertook the housework and the ironing, and Emily baked the bread and attended to the kitchen. Charlotte declared that she was happier black-leading the stoves, sweeping the floors, and making the beds at home than she would be "living like a fine lady" anywhere else.

During that winter she wrote a novelette, and in the summer of 1840 she was reading a bundle of French books, forty volumes, sent her by the Taylors—"clever, sophistical, immoral." Early in 1841 she was in another situation, this time as nursery governess with the Whites, at Upperwood House, Rawdon—only a few

"QUALIFIED TO TEACH" 51

miles from Ellen Nussey and the Rydings. They were kindly people, and evidently liked and trusted their little governess. "By dint of nursing the fat baby," wrote Charlotte, "it has got to know me, and to be fond of me. I suspect myself of growing rather fond of it."

Anne had left Mirfield, and was governess with the Robinsons, at Thorp Green. She was not happy there, and Charlotte was very anxious about Anne's health. A scheme was on foot for the girls to set up a school of their own. Miss Wooler had proposed their taking over her old school at Dewsbury Moor, but there were reasons against this. It was not so prosperous as it had been, and would require " working up "; and the sisters began to realise that they did not know enough themselves. What did they know of foreign languages and music ? And how, without them, could they hope to keep a school, or to command high salaries as governesses in private families ? They were very undecided what to do, when a long letter from Mary Taylor, and a packet enclosing " a very handsome black silk scarf and a pair of very beautiful kid gloves, bought at Brussels," changed the whole course of Charlotte Brontë's life. They came to her while she was still with the Whites, at Rawdon. Her mind was in a ferment. Mary's letter had brought with it visions of " pictures the most exquisite, and cathedrals the most venerable, . . . all the excitements of one of the most splendid capitals of Europe."

It had also pointed out a possible path for Charlotte and her sisters. She took her courage in her two hands, and wrote to the only person in the world who was able to help them—to Aunt Branwell.

Charlotte's letter set before her aunt in very vigorous language the advantages to be gained if she and Emily were given a half-year at a school in Brussels. It would cost £50, or £100, but it would be the making of them for life. " Papa will perhaps think it a wild and ambitious scheme ; but who ever rose in the world without ambition ? When he left Ireland to go to Cambridge

University, he was as ambitious as I am now. I want us *all* to get on. I know we have talents, and I want them to be turned to account. I look to you, aunt, to help us. I think you will not refuse. I know if you consent, it shall not be my fault if you ever repent your kindness." [1]

After some hesitation and a good deal of talk, the dear old lady gave her consent, and she did it handsomely too, for she not only advanced the £50, but she said she would like to pay extra, so that the girls might have a separate bedroom for themselves. The parson and Aunt Branwell were at first inclined to Lille, in preference to Brussels; but at last a school was found in Brussels—the *pensionnat* of Madame Héger, in the Rue d'Isabelle, recommended by the chaplain to the British Embassy. And so, at Christmas 1841, Charlotte bade good-bye to her kind employers, and to the fat baby whom she had grown to love. The Brontë family were once more together for Christmas. Charlotte and Emily were busy preparing their simple wardrobes for the Brussels visit; Anne was to stay at home and take care of "papa and aunt."

Early in 1840, Branwell Brontë had gone as private tutor to a family at Broughton-in-Furness. "How he will like to settle remains yet to be seen," wrote Charlotte to Ellen Nussey; "at present he is full of hope and resolution. I, who know his variable nature and his strong turn for active life, dare not be too sanguine. We are as busy as possible in preparing for his departure, and shirt-making and collar-stitching fully occupy our time." [2]

How Branwell Brontë "settled" in Mr. Postlethwaite's household, and how much Charlotte Brontë knew about her brother's "variable" nature, may be learned from a long letter, often quoted, which he wrote from Broughton-in-Furness to John Brown, the sexton at home. It is certainly a silly letter, full of pose and swagger, but it is vicious, hypocritical, and unutterably selfish. It was thought a wonderful production by "Old Knave of

[1] Mrs. Gaskell's *Life*. [2] Sir Wemyss Reid's *Monograph*.

PENSIONNAT HÉGER

Trumps" (the sexton), and "Little Nosey" (the landlord of the Black Bull), and the rest of the fraternity. They read it so often that they came to know it by heart.

Branwell did not keep Mr. Postlethwaite's situation very long. He obtained the post of railway clerk, at first at Sowerby Bridge, and then at Luddenden Foot, on the new Leeds and Manchester Railway; and when Charlotte and Emily were starting for Brussels he had not been at home for some months, and it was hoped he was getting on pretty well.

CHAPTER IX

PENSIONNAT HÉGER

A QUAINT-LOOKING little trio they must have been, setting out from the parsonage, on a February day in 1842—little Charlotte, and the lank Emily, and the parson cravatted up to the chin. For the parson had expressed his intention of taking his two daughters to Brussels. Somewhere on the way to London they were joined by Mary Taylor and one of her brothers, both of whom were accustomed to travelling, which the parson was not. As for the Brontë sisters, they had never been out of Yorkshire before, except to go to Cowan Bridge School, though Charlotte had certainly "seen the sea" when Ellen Nussey had taken her for a fortnight to Easton.

The travellers put up at the old Chapter Coffee-house in Paternoster Row, and during the day or two they spent in London before sailing in the Ostend packet from London Bridge wharf, they visited St. Paul's, and saw "all the pictures and statues" they could in London.

It was dark when they arrived in Brussels, and the girls were separated, Mary to go to her more expensive school at the Château de Koekelberg, and Charlotte and Emily to be handed over by the parson to the care

54   THE BRONTËS

of Madame Héger in the Rue d'Isabelle. Mr. Brontë stayed one night with the English chaplain, and then travelled straight back to Haworth.

The sisters—Charlotte nearly twenty-six, and Emily only two years younger—found themselves schoolgirls again. "All the excitements of one of the most splendid capitals of Europe" lay outside the walled garden of that old house in the Rue d'Isabelle, but the girls could have seen and heard but little of them all. They were there for work, hard work. They found themselves almost the only Protestants in a large school of boarders and day-pupils—about ninety all told. Masters came and went, to teach all sorts of subjects. Mademoiselle This and Mademoiselle That flitted about the school with light feet, looking after the young ladies, and doing Madame's bidding. M. and Madame Héger, with their children, lived in the school. Madame was head of the school, and Monsieur was professor of rhetoric. He taught also at the boys' school hard by—the Athénée Royal de Bruxelles. Charlotte and Emily soon found that the difference of nationality and religion made "a broad line of demarcation" between them and the rest of the school. "We are completely isolated in the midst of numbers," wrote Charlotte. They clung together—in the classroom they sat side by side, absorbed in their work; in the garden they paced silently up and down together, Emily leaning on her smaller elder sister. Everything was new and strange to them—the *refectoire*, with its foreign cookery; the *oratoire*, with its crucifix; the shady garden, with its *allée défendue;* the *lecture pieuse* at night, which the little ultra-Protestants hated; the foreign names and voices in the streets; the bell of S. Gudule. They were learning, learning, from morning till night; but both were quite well. Emily worked like a horse.

Madame was an admirable head of a school—calm, cool, and self-possessed. She struck Charlotte as being rather like Miss Wooler, only married. They saw more of M. Héger, because he was their teacher. "A man of power, as to mind," wrote Charlotte. "but of a very choleric and irritable temperament." She was not sure at first if she liked him ; and as for Emily, " Emily and he don't draw well together at all." M. Héger, however, was an enthusiast in his subject, and Charlotte and Emily—enthusiasts too—were soon deep in their *devoirs* for him. Mrs. Gaskell has preserved some of these, with the marginal comments of the professor. And surely never did a pupil's *devoirs* show more care and thought and effort than do these little French prose-essays of Charlotte Brontë's ; and never did professorial marginal notes stand out more vehemently characteristic of the man who made them.

The silent Emily was headstrong, prejudiced, and often homesick ; her English Protestantism recoiled from the " gentle Jesuitry " about her. Charlotte was more docile : she was, in fact, very happy. " It felt very strange at first," she wrote home, " to submit to authority instead of exercising it, to obey orders instead of giving them ; but I like that state of things."

It was true that the professor's face, in moments of academic wrath, could suddenly take on the expression of " an insane tom-cat " or " a delirious hyæna " ; but he could be also mild, and of a great courtesy towards his two English pupils, whom he recognised as women of strong character and extraordinary ability—women whom he could teach as he would not have dreamed of teaching the ordinary Belgian girls of the Pensionnat Héger. Charlotte began to like and admire the little choleric professor of rhetoric. For the first time in her secluded life she found herself in the society of a man between whom and herself there was a strong intellectual sympathy. Her whole ambition in coming to Brussels had been to learn to teach : she now began to understand what might be the meaning of the words master and pupil.

When their six months came to an end, Madame Héger proposed that Charlotte and Emily should stay on for another half-year as pupil-teachers, without paying, but without salary. They accepted the proposal, but they were not to make out their year. That autumn, Martha Taylor—"Little Miss Boisterous"—was taken suddenly ill at the Château de Koekelberg, and died in a few days. She was buried in the English cemetery outside Brussels; and even while, shocked and saddened, the girls were making their first pilgrimages to Martha's new grave in the "heretic" cemetery, word came from Haworth that Aunt Branwell was ill. Charlotte and Emily immediately packed up to go home, and, just as they were starting, a second letter came to say that she was dead. Travelling day and night, they could not reach home in time for the funeral, and when they did arrive, it was all over, and "Mr. Brontë and Anne were sitting together in quiet grief."[1]

Aunt Branwell had been buried, by her own wish, as near as possible to her sister. Her little fortune, about £1500, had been left between her three nieces and a fourth niece in Penzance. In her will—made so long before as 1833—she had left her "Indian workbox" to Charlotte, her ivory fan and her "workbox with the china lid" to Emily, her "japan dressing-box" to Branwell, and to Anne, whom she had reared from a baby, her gold watch, and "all that belonged to it." The little gold snuffbox was not mentioned; but the eyeglass that had played so dear a part in the literary life of the family, with its chain, and her rings, and books, and silver spoons, were all to be divided among her three nieces, "as their father shall think proper." And now she was gone—the little figure in the silk gown and the mob-cap, with the auburn curls on the forehead; the little figure that for nearly twenty years had clicked about in her pattens on the stone-flagged floors of the parsonage, and longed for the sunshine and society of Penzance.

And somebody else was gone too. Poor Mr. Weightman, the curate, was dead, after a very short illness. The parson had preached the funeral sermon on October 2nd—the first sermon he had read for more than twenty years. For "the ordinary run of hearers," Mr. Brontë

[1] Mrs. Gaskell's *Life*.

PENSIONNAT HÉGER

preferred extempore preaching, but on this occasion he wrote his sermon with some care; and it was printed, by request, and sold for sixpence a copy—the profits, "if any," to go to the Sunday-school. So poor Anne's little romance—if a romance it ever was—was over. There would be no more valentines, no more verses beginning, "Away, fond Love!" and "Soul Divine!" Aunt, Martha Taylor, and Mr. Weightman were all gone, and the world seemed "dreary and void."

After Christmas—a snowy Christmas up on the moors—Anne returned to Thorp Green; and it was arranged that Branwell, who was back on their hands again, should go with her, as tutor to the son of the family. Branwell had left his post of railway clerk at Luddenden Foot; he had also left the company's accounts in a state of muddle, and Mr. Brontë had, as usual, to make good his son's defalcations. It is difficult to understand how, even then, the family could think of saddling poor Anne with the ne'er-do-weel.

M. Héger wrote to Mr. Brontë a letter full of praises of "*nos deux chères élèves*"—pupils such as Madame and he had had very little experience of before, and whom they were very sorry to lose. He pressed the parson to allow at least one of the young ladies to return, and he set before him the advantages offered by a second year at the *pensionnat*. They would study German. Emily would have lessons from the best music-master in Belgium; Charlotte, as English teacher, would be learning to teach *in French*. Both would be put in the way of gaining "*cette douce indépendance si difficile à trouver pour une jeune personne.*"

But Emily, once at home again, had no wish to go back to the Pensionnat Héger; and it was arranged that, as Anne and Branwell were to be at Thorp Green, Emily should keep house for the parson, and Charlotte should be the one to return to Brussels. She was to have a salary of £16, out of which she was to pay for her German lessons.

It was January when Charlotte started alone on her

journey. From Euston, she drove straight down to London Bridge wharf, hired a waterman to row her out to the Ostend packet, slept on board, and sailed next morning. After three days' travelling she found herself once more in the Rue d'Isabelle, where Madame Héger received her "with great kindness."

She was soon initiated into her new duties. She was now "Mademoiselle Charlotte," teacher of English; and a very unruly and boisterous set of Belgian girls she had to teach. But she rose to the occasion. "A slight increase of colour, a momentary sparkling of the eye, and more decided energy of manner were the only outward tokens she gave." She declined all offers of help from Monsieur and Madame, and set about the task of managing her pupils in her own quiet way. And —the rôles of pupil and teacher being reversed—she gave lessons in English to M. Héger and M. Chapelle, his brother-in-law.

Why was it that Charlotte Brontë was so unhappy during this second year at Brussels? What happened to make it such a failure?

"I returned to Brussels after aunt's death," she said at a later period, "against my conscience, prompted by what then seemed an irresistible impulse. I was punished for my selfish folly by a total withdrawal, for more than two years, of happiness and peace of mind."

People at home, at the time, had a theory that there was an attachment in Brussels. Her biographers have put forth various theories on the subject of her return to Brussels and her unhappiness during this second year there. It was her ultra-Protestantism that estranged her from Madame, a devout Catholic; her habitual aloofness, which prevented her from making friends with the other governesses in the house. She missed the presence of Emily, and Mary, and poor little Martha; her intellectual solitude preyed on her nerves, and made her emotional and morbid; ugly accounts of Branwell's misdoings were always filtering through the home-letters, and there were other anxieties at the parsonage—anxieties that exaggerated themselves in the long, sleepless nights of the summer *vacances* in the big empty *pensionnat*.

Some of these theories Charlotte herself has dealt with. She smiled, at first, at the people who could not understand that she crossed the sea merely to return as teacher to Madame Héger's school, " out of respect for my master and mistress, and gratitude for their kindness." If only people knew how secluded was her life at the school—how she never exchanged a word with any other man than M. Héger, and seldom, now that she was no longer a pupil, even with him! And then, as the months go on, she is convinced that Madame Héger no longer likes her—why, she cannot tell, and she does not believe that Madame has any definite reason. M. Héger is much influenced by Madame, and he reads Mademoiselle Charlotte a lecture on her want of *bienveillance*. She comes to think Madame Héger politic, plausible, and interested; she no longer trusts her. Except the loss of M. Héger's goodwill—if, indeed, she has lost that—she cares for nothing. He has always been kind to her, "loading her with books," so that she has owed to him all the pleasures she has in her life.[1]

Sir Wemyss Reid says that Charlotte Brontë went back to Brussels because " her spirit, if not her heart," had been " captured and held captive in the Belgian city." According to him, this second visit to Brussels changed her whole life's current, and gave it " a new purpose and a new meaning." *Shirley*, he says, might have been written if Charlotte Brontë had never gone back to Brussels, but *Jane Eyre* and *Villette* never. And the lesson she learnt there, which made it possible for her to write these books that gripped at the heart-strings of the whole reading world, was the self-knowledge that is as bitter in the mouth as it is whole-some to the life. That is Sir Wemyss Reid's theory; and it must, in addition, be remembered that this lesson of self-knowledge which Charlotte Brontë learnt was also the only lesson which circumstances obliged

[1] Mr. Clement Shorter's *Charlotte Brontë and her Circle*.

her to learn without the services of a master. And those who knew her in her lifetime, and those who have studied her character in her writings and her own intimate letters, are absolutely agreed that little Charlotte Brontë—romantic enthusiast as she was, liable to moods of deepest depression and of strong emotional exaltation—was also a small warrior of indomitable courage, who, in her own slender hands, held the standard of truth and honour very high.

In the autumn of 1843, during the *grandes vacances*, when the school was emptied, the Hégers and their children were away on holiday, and only the French governess, whom she detested, was left to keep her company in the Rue d'Isabelle, Charlotte Brontë had certainly worked herself into a state of great nervous tension. She had little to occupy her. It was a fine hot September; for hours together she "tramped about" the boulevards and streets of Brussels.

One long September day she went on a solitary pilgrimage to little Martha's grave in the Protestant cemetery; and from there she walked on, far beyond it, till she reached the top of a hill, from which she could look down on a landscape of green fields stretching away to the horizon. It was a long walk back into the town again, and it was evening when she found herself, tired and faint, in the busy streets of Brussels. Still she felt a nervous dread of returning to the Rue d'Isabelle and to the big empty school. The bell of S. Gudule was tolling for vespers; she slipped in under the big doorway, and found herself in the silent, incense-sweetened gloom of the cathedral aisles, where only a few old women were kneeling in prayer. She stayed through vespers, and when they were over she still lingered on. A few people were kneeling at the confessionals, and an "odd whim" came into her head: she did not care what she did, so long as it was not really wrong. She watched the penitents confessing, and after a few minutes she too knelt down on the steps before one of the gratings of a confessional. When the grating opened, and the priest turned his ear towards

PENSIONNAT HÉGER 61

her, she did not know how to begin. She did not know the formula of a confession, and was obliged to say that she was a Protestant. The priest was at first unwilling to grant her the privilege of confession, but after a moment or two of parleying he did allow her to confess ; and in her letter to Emily, describing this whole day, she says that she did actually confess—" a real confession." He asked her to come next day to his own house, that he might try by reasoning to convert her ; and she promised at the moment. But there her little adventure stopped ; she never saw the priest again. After all, it was only " a freak." [1]

Whim, or freak, or whatever it was, this long day, ending at the little wooden grating in the dusk of the confessional in S. Gudule, may have formulated the troubled thoughts and feelings of the solitary little woman. The penitent hears the confession as well as the priest. That was in September. In October, when the school was reopened, she gave Madame Héger notice, and " if it had depended on her " she would have gone then ; but M. Héger sent for her, and " pronounced with vehemence his decision that I should not leave," and she promised to stay on a little longer. Through November, home affairs were filling her heart. Her father's eyesight was failing ; more of the work of the parish was devolving on the curate ; and, Mr. Weightman being dead, the curate was new. There was no longer Aunt Branwell at hand, with her little gold eye-glass, to read to Mr. Brontë out of the *Leeds Intelligencer* and *Blackwood's Magazine*. The " fighting gentry " had come about him, the more convivial of them with their late hours, their talk, and their whisky-toddy ; and the poor old parson, so long almost a stoic in the simplicity of his life, was drinking a great deal more whisky than was good for him.

Charlotte could not tell the Hégers all that was on her mind, but her father's growing blindness was reason enough. In December she gave up her post ; and on January 2, 1844, armed with " a kind of diploma,"

[1] Mr. Clement Shorter's *Charlotte Brontë and her Circle*.

signed by M. Héger, and sealed with the seal of the Athénée Royal de Bruxelles, of which he was professor, she arrived at the parsonage.

"I suffered much before I left Brussels. I think, however long I live, I shall not forget what the parting with M. Héger cost me; it grieved me so much to grieve him, who has been so true, kind, and disinterested a friend. . . . There are times now when it appears to me as if all my ideas and feelings, except a few friendships and affections, are changed from what they used to be: something in me, which used to be enthusiasm, is tamed down and broken. I have fewer illusions; what I wish for now is active exertion—a stake in life." [1]

CHAPTER X

CURRER, ELLIS, AND ACTON BELL

CHARLOTTE took Aunt Branwell's place in the grey old parsonage, and with his eldest daughter's home-coming the parson resumed, once for all, his old abstemious habits of life.

Charlotte and Emily, with Emily's big bulldog at her heels, tramped the moors, and laid their plans for setting up a school of their own under the parsonage roof. They actually printed a circular, announcing the existence of "The Misses Brontë's Establishment for the Board and Education of a Limited Number of Young Ladies." The pupils were to be charged £35 a year; the "extras" were to consist of the hard-won French and German, with Latin (was "papa" to teach that?), music, and drawing. Each young lady was to bring with her sheets, pillow-cases, towels, and two spoons—nobody knows why not also a knife and fork. The sisters even talked of the alterations that would be needed at the parsonage; but month after month passed, and not one single pupil applied.

[1] Mrs. Gaskell's *Life*.

Mr. Brontë was now so nearly blind that he was led up the steps into his pulpit. His congregation found the old man's extempore sermons as forcible as ever, and they noticed that from old habit he ended exactly at the half-hour, though he could no longer see the clock in front of his pulpit. He was often in very low spirits, for he was afraid that as his blindness increased he should become "nothing in his parish." But this was no longer the turbulent Irishman of youthful days; he was never impatient, "only anxious and dejected."

The Taylor family had lost money, and Mary Taylor had gone out to New Zealand, with one of her brothers, and set up there on her own account, in "a small drapery business." Ellen Nussey was keeping house for her brother Henry; but in the summer of 1845 Charlotte's old admirer, Henry Nussey, was married, and while he was on his honeymoon Charlotte stayed with Ellen at his Derbyshire vicarage. There might have been a more exhilarating holiday than a visit to the house of an old admirer while he was away being married to somebody else; but it was a very happy time—the last happy time that Charlotte was to spend for many a long day. When she returned home, Branwell was at the parsonage, "very ill."

This time Branwell had positively excelled himself. It was evident that he had been drinking again; but his latest achievement had been to make love to the wife of his employer. The lady had told her husband, the tutor was "sternly dismissed," and of course poor Anne, the most deserving of governesses, was obliged to pack her box and follow her brother.

The interior of the parsonage may be imagined. "He will do nothing but drink, and make us all wretched," wrote poor Charlotte. They tried to prevent his drinking by keeping him without money, but he found opium "more portable and more effectual" than whisky or gin. His plausibility and his eloquence of self-pity played upon their feelings, and, with a dipsomaniac's low cunning, he managed to trick them all. To the very end his sisters more than half believed his whining story. He wrote weak poetry; he wrote letters—profusely illustrated with sketches of himself undergoing various forms of bodily and mental torture—to the one or two companions of his portrait-painting, railway-clerking days; he talked grandiosely at the Black Bull, and he babbled, "in confidence," to every one who would listen to him; but it was all one long tissue of lies—the lies of the opium-eater.

There is preserved a part of one of Charlotte Brontë's French letters to M. Héger, written at this time,[1] written with all the care of one of her old *devoirs*. She tells him that if she could write a book, she would dedicate it to "*Mon maître de litterature, au seul maître que j'aie jamais eu—à vous, Monsieur!*" But she is afraid that will never be: "*Il ne faut pas y penser. La carrière des lettres m'est fermée.*"

But the darkest hour comes before the dawn. Charlotte Brontë came accidentally one day on a little manuscript volume of poetry in Emily's handwriting. Anne thereupon brought her poems to be looked at; and the three sisters—for Charlotte also had been guilty of writing poetry—agreed to publish a volume of their collected verses. They decided to assume the names of "Currer, Ellis, and Acton Bell." They did not wish to claim "positively masculine" names; but they had noticed that reviewers had a sort of prejudice against women's work, an objectionable manner both of criticising and of praising women. So they kept their own initials, and chose names that might belong to either men or women. They wrote to several publishers without getting any answer at all; but at last, in the spring of 1846, "Currer, Ellis, and Acton Bell" had placed their little volume with Messrs. Aylott & Jones of Paternoster Row. It was to be published at the authors' expense, and cost them £31, 10s. Aylott & Jones were by no means well-known publishers—in fact they had scarcely published anything at all—but that mattered little so long as they were going to publish the works of Currer, Ellis, and Acton Bell. Great was

[1] Mrs. Gaskell's *Life*.

the satisfaction of the sisters in all the preliminary details of type and paper. The publishers knew them only as "three persons, relatives," and the £31, 10s. was duly received at Paternoster Row. In April, the little volume—a much thinner volume than they had expected—appeared. The editor of *Blackwood's Magazine*, of course, received a presentation copy, and so did eight or ten other magazines and newspapers of the day—most of them now extinct. The *Dublin University Magazine* gave the book such a good review that "Currer Bell" was moved to write and thank that periodical; and the *Athenæum* also gave them a notice under "Poetry for the Million." The *Athenæum* praised Emily's poems most, Charlotte's came next, and Anne's followed meekly in the wake. By July, Messrs. Aylott & Jones reported *two copies* sold; and one of these must have been read by somebody, for a gentleman in Warwick had actually written, through the publishers, to ask for the autographs of the "Messrs. Bell." The sisters began to feel the thrill of excitement that comes with writing books. Already each was engaged on a prose work—a work of fiction. They had fallen back on their old habit of sitting up late, and pacing up and down the parsonage dining-room. Each had worked out a plot, and talked it into shape; and now the three novels were nearly finished. The great difficulty was to find any publisher who would undertake, at his own expense, to publish three works of fiction by three unknown authors—always supposing, of course, that he liked the works of fiction after he had seen them. Messrs. Aylott & Jones politely refused; it was not exactly in their way.

For months the manuscripts were sent about, at first together, and then separately. Charlotte had called hers *The Professor*, Emily's was *Wuthering Heights*, and Anne's was *Agnes Grey*.

Charlotte Brontë used to tell afterwards how *The Professor* had come back from one of its journeys by post just as she and her father were starting for Manchester, where Mr. Brontë was to be operated on for cataract. Charlotte and Emily had already been to Manchester to see the oculist, Mr. Wilson; and in August 1846 Charlotte and her father were settled in their Manchester lodgings. The old parson proved a real Spartan, and the operation was very successful. All went well, and in September father and daughter were back at the parsonage again. Mr. Brontë was not allowed to use his eyes much. Branwell had behaved pretty well during their absence.

The winter set in very cold at Haworth, and—the three novels were still going the round of the publishers—the sisters were feeling nipped and dull. "Nothing happens at Haworth," wrote Charlotte; and then she remembered that something had happened "to sting us to life." A sheriff's officer had arrived for Branwell. Branwell must either pay his debts or "take a trip to York." And, of course, the debts were paid.

While Charlotte was in the lodgings at Manchester she had begun another novel. On one of those evenings at the parsonage, when the sisters walked up and down the dining-room, they had discussed their heroines. Charlotte maintained that the other two were "morally wrong" in making heroines always beautiful. Emily and Anne thought heroines could not be interesting unless they were beautiful; and then Charlotte had broken out, with some passion:

"I will prove to you that you are wrong. I will show you a heroine as plain and as small as myself, who shall be as interesting as any of yours." And so, in that Manchester lodging, while the parson lay in his darkened room, Charlotte Brontë, with a pencil and loose sheets of paper, as was her wont, writing on her knee, against a piece of board or broken book-cover, had begun to write *Jane Eyre*.

The story of the publication of *Jane Eyre* is one of the gold nuggets of literary history. *The Professor* had been sent, "as a forlorn hope," to Messrs. Smith & Elder, in Cornhill. It was characteristic of Charlotte Brontë that she had sent it in the same old paper wrapping in which it had made its journeys to and from all the other publishers who had rejected it. Their names were merely scored out, but were quite legible.

Messrs. Smith & Elder returned the manuscript,[1] but with it came a letter so courteous and so kind, a letter containing such wise criticism and advice, that it in itself made up for the disappointment of a refusal. And the letter held out a hope. If the writer of *The Professor* would send them a three-volumed novel, Messrs. Smith & Elder would give it their careful consideration.

And *Jane Eyre* was already half finished ! On August 24, 1847, the precious manuscript was sent off by rail. Everybody knows how Mr. Williams—Messrs. Smith & Elder's literary adviser—read it first ; and how Mr. Smith was "much amused" by Mr. Williams's unbounded enthusiasm ; and how Mr. James Taylor—who, being a Scotsman, was not supposed to be of an enthusiastic temperament at all—read it next, and sat up half the night to finish it ; and how at last Mr. Smith read it himself, and agreed with them both that it was a wonderful book.

After some correspondence and much proof-correcting —for " C. Bell " had apparently not punctuated his manuscript at all correctly—Messrs. Smith & Elder published *Jane Eyre, an Autobiography, edited by " Currer Bell."* A day or two later six presentation copies arrived at the parsonage, and " C. Bell " wrote off to 65 Cornhill : " You have given the work every advantage which good paper, clear type, and a seemly outside can supply. If it fails, the fault will lie with the author ; you are exempt. I now await the judgment of the press and the public."

And everybody knows what that judgment was. From that day there was a constant coming and going of letters and literary notices between the house in Cornhill and the parsonage at Haworth. Charlotte Brontë was triumphantly launched on that "*carrière des lettres*" which, so short a time before, had seemed so impossible to her. But all the time nobody, in Corn-

[1] *The Professor* was not published till after Charlotte Brontë's death.

hill or anywhere else—not even Ellen Nussey—knew who "C. Bell" was—whether man or woman; and when the Haworth postman asked Mr. Brontë who the "Currer Bell" could be for whom so many letters came, the parson assured him there was no person of that name in the parish. For some time Mr. Brontë had been "silently cognisant" that his daughters were doing something in the literary line. It could scarcely have been otherwise, with three daughters and four novels, and pen and ink and paper all over the parsonage. But Charlotte's moment of triumph came on the day when, just after "papa" had finished his early dinner, she walked into his study with the three volumes of *Jane Eyre* in her hand, and one or two carefully selected reviews of the book, some good and one bad. Mrs. Gaskell heard the story from Charlotte Brontë's own lips, and wrote it down at the time: [1]

"Papa, I've been writing a book."

"Have you, my dear?"

"Yes; and I want you to read it."

"I am afraid it will try my eyes too much."

"But it is not in manuscript; it is printed."

And then, of course, the poor old parson's first thought was the expense. Had Charlotte thought of that? It would be almost sure to be a loss. But little Charlotte quietly unfolded some of the reviews.

"But, papa, I don't think it will be a loss; no more will you, if you will just let me read you a review or two and tell you more about it."

Then she left him alone with *Jane Eyre;* and when he came out of his study at tea-time, he uttered the memorable paternal benediction, so often quoted, "Girls, do you know Charlotte has been writing a book, and *it is much better than likely?*"

The "girls" shared their sister's triumph. Their novels too had been accepted some little time before this by a Mr. Newby of Mortimer Street, Cavendish Square, and were to be published together, in three volumes—Emily's in the first two, and Anne's in the

[1] Mrs. Gaskell's *Life*.

third volume. Mr. Newby, however, was not like Messrs. Smith & Elder, and it was only after much vexatious delay that *Wuthering Heights* and *Agnes Grey* appeared, in December 1847. Unlike *Jane Eyre*, they made no sensation in the literary world.

And what of Branwell Brontë all this time ? It is difficult to understand, but Charlotte Brontë has left it on record that Branwell knew nothing of the publication of these novels. His condition had been going from bad to worse. His story—long ago proved to have been the hallucination of a disordered brain—was that when his " enemy " died he was to marry the widow ; and he wrote and talked largely of the day when he should come into possession of " herself and estate." But in May 1846 his " enemy " did die, and then his story changed : the marriage was impossible because the " estate " had been left in such a way that the whole of it would be forfeited by a second marriage. A horseman was said to have brought this unwelcome news to Branwell at the Black Bull. Exactly what did happen inside the parlour of the Black Bull Inn was never divulged ; but the Haworth villagers said that, when the horseman rode away, he left Branwell Brontë " bleating like a calf."

At times the parsonage must have been like a lunatic asylum. Branwell slept in his father's room, and in his fits of delirium he more than once threatened to kill the brave old man, who, half blind as he was, would allow no one else to wrestle with his son. The sisters, lying awake, would listen in terror for the report of a pistol, or a dull, heavy thud on the floor. And in the morning Branwell would come down to breakfast with his, " The poor old man and I have had a terrible night of it. He does his best, the poor old man, but it's all over with me ! "

Charlotte warned Ellen Nussey, when she came to stay at the parsonage in August 1847, that she must expect to find Branwell changed in appearance, that he was " broken in mind." And to somewhere about this time belongs the description from the pen of Mr. Grundy, his friend of the railway-station days. Mr. Grundy had come to Haworth to see Branwell. He had ordered dinner for two at the Black Bull, and had sent up a message to the parsonage.

"Whilst I waited his appearance, his father was shown in. Much of the Rector's old stiffness of manner was gone. He spoke of Branwell with more affection than I had ever heretofore heard him express; but he also spoke almost hopelessly."

The parson had only come to explain that his son was in bed ill, but that he had insisted on dressing and coming, and would be there immediately.

"Presently the door opened cautiously, and a head appeared. It was a mass of red, unkempt, uncut hair, wildly floating round a great gaunt forehead, the cheeks yellow and hollow, the mouth fallen, the thin white lips not trembling but shaking, the sunken eyes, once small, now glaring with the light of madness. . ."[1]

This was the handsome boy, the pride of the family. Almost in despair, Charlotte writes, in January 1848: "Papa is harassed day and night; we have little peace; he is always sick; has two or three times fallen down in fits. What will be the ultimate end, God knows."

CHAPTER XI

THE VALLEY OF THE SHADOW

In April 1848 *Jane Eyre* was in a third edition, and was having "a great run" in America. More often than ever did the Haworth postman bring letters for "Mr. Currer Bell, care of Miss Brontë." There were welcome "remittances," too, of £100 at a time, from Messrs. Smith & Elder; and Mr. Williams, their literary adviser, who was the first to read *Jane Eyre*, wrote regularly to "Mr. Currer Bell." With his delightful letters came the newspaper and magazine notices as they

[1] Leyland.

THE VALLEY OF THE SHADOW 71

appeared, and all sorts of new books—gifts from the firm in Cornhill. And all the time nobody at Cornhill knew whether " Currer Bell," the author of *Jane Eyre*, was man or woman.

Meantime, *Wuthering Heights* and *Agnes Grey*, so awkwardly linked together, were by no means setting the Thames on fire. Emily and Anne had advanced £50 on their venture, and were not getting anything back from Mr. Newby. But Anne had written another novel, and in June 1848 Mr. Newby, apparently on the chance of a popularity reflected from *Jane Eyre*, published *The Tenant of Wildfell Hall, by Acton Bell*, in three volumes. For this, Anne received £25 on the day of publication, and was to receive another £25 when 250 copies should be sold. Poor Emily, therefore, whose strange, wild genius was to raise her afterwards on a pedestal of her very own, was so far the only one of the trio whose work had met with no recognition.

It was a week or two after the appearance of *The Tenant of Wildfell Hall*—one Friday early in July 1848—that the letter arrived from Messrs. Smith & Elder which caused such consternation at the parsonage. The American publisher of *Jane Eyre* had bargained for early sheets of the next novel by Currer Bell; but it now appeared that a rival American firm was advertising an edition of *The Tenant of Wildfell Hall* as being by the author of *Jane Eyre*, and that Mr. Newby was assuring people that Currer, Ellis, and Acton Bell were really one and the same person, and that Acton Bell's new novel was likely to eclipse *Jane Eyre*. Here was a situation for the sisters! Charlotte and Anne decided that they must go up to London at once, to " prove their separate identity " ; and thus did the famous week-end in London come about, so graphically described by Mrs. Gaskell. Mr. Clement Shorter has preserved Charlotte Brontë's letter to Mary Taylor in New Zealand, from which Mrs. Gaskell took her account.[1]

That very Friday, after tea, Charlotte and Anne set off on foot to Keighley, were overtaken by a thunder-

[1] Mr. Clement Shorter's *Charlotte Brontë and her Circle*.

storm—with snow, in July!—just managed to catch the train to Leeds, and from Leeds were "whirled up to London by the night train." Of course they put up at the Chapter Coffee-house — "our old place, Polly," wrote Charlotte to Mary Taylor. No ladies ever went to the Chapter Coffee-house; it was an inn frequented by booksellers, and now and then by a clergyman, like their father, from the country. But the old waiter made them as comfortable as he could, and after breakfast they sallied forth on foot to find No. 65 Cornhill.

The two little women, "in queer inward excitement," entered the big bookseller's shop and asked to speak to Mr. Smith. There was some hesitation, for the ladies had withheld their names; but at last they were "shown up," and Mr. Smith, a tall young man, standing in a small room, lighted by a great skylight, saw approaching him two demure-looking little women, one of whom, looking up at him through her spectacles, placed in his hands his own letter to "Mr. Currer Bell" —the letter that had arrived at the parsonage the day before.

The tall young man looked at the letter, and then again at the two little women.

"*Where did you get this?*" he asked, in evident perplexity, and Charlotte Brontë, still looking up at him through her spectacles, could not help laughing.

"A recognition took place." This, then, was Currer Bell! *this* was the author of *Jane Eyre!*

Mr. Williams was fetched immediately, and Charlotte saw, in the "pale, mild, stooping man of fifty," the man who had first read her, and discovered her, and made her fame and fortune, with whom she had ever since been corresponding so delightfully. Little wonder that there was more recognition, and a "long, nervous shaking of hands." It was a good thing that they all had the enormities of Mr. Newby to fall back upon.

The days that followed seemed like a dream. Nothing could have been more kind and hospitable than Mr. George Smith and his mother and sisters. There was

THE VALLEY OF THE SHADOW 73

the visit to the opera, to hear Rossini's *Barber of Seville*, when Charlotte and Anne, in their homely, high-necked gowns, found themselves on the great crimson staircase of the Opera House, amid the " gracefully supercilious " wealth and fashion of a London season ; and Charlotte could not help slightly pressing Mr. Williams's arm and whispering, " *You know I am not accustomed to this sort of thing.*" There was the Sunday morning service in a London city church, with Mr. Williams as escort, and the rather nervous dinner at Mr. Smith's " splendid " house in Bayswater ; and on Monday there were the pictures at the National Gallery and the Royal Academy, and dinner again in Bayswater, and an evening visit to Mr. Williams's house, to see his " fine family of eight."

On Tuesday, " laden with books," they were whirled away again, and, very tired, very excited and happy, found themselves once more at home, in the old parsonage, embedded in the moors. Only the kindly publishers were in their secret ; to the world at large the sisters were still " Currer, Ellis, and Acton Bell " ; and during the London visit Charlotte and Anne had passed as " the Miss Browns."

That summer Branwell Brontë was very ill. His conduct was much the same, but his constitution was shattered. August and September passed miserably. Nobody at the parsonage—not even the doctors who had been called in—realised how near the end was. Branwell was in the village on September 22nd, and he died on the 24th.

" We have hurried our dead out of our sight," wrote Charlotte to the sympathetic Mr. Williams. The old parson, now that it was all over, was " acutely distressed " ; and the sisters, after three years of a life that was like a nightmare to look back upon, told each other that Branwell had been more his old innocent self during those last two days of his life.

At the time of Branwell's death, Emily and Anne were both ill—both were, in fact, victims of the disease that had carried off the two little sisters nearly twenty years before. Emily Brontë sank rapidly. She never left the parsonage after the Sunday following her brother's death, and in less than three months—before the year was out—she too was dead.

"The spirit was inexorable to the flesh," says Charlotte of this sister. She had inherited the parson's physical courage and his obduracy. In the old days, when they had dubbed her "the Major," it was Emily who, in her eccentric fashion, had stood between them and the little disagreeables of life, on whom the household duties had fallen heaviest as "Tabby" grew old and infirm. It was Emily who cared for the animals— the dogs, the geese, and the tame hawk, "Hero." Many are the stories of Emily's Spartan self-discipline. Once, when a strange dog bit her hand, she went into the parsonage kitchen and, without alarming any one, seared her own wound with a red-hot iron. When the sisters, going upstairs one night, saw flames coming out of Branwell's room, it was Emily who had the presence of mind to extinguish the fire with pails of water, without waking the parson. It was Emily who quelled her bulldog into obedience with her own bare fist, and then herself tenderly fomented his poor old swollen head. During those last dark years it had always been Emily who was "strong enough" to sit up for Branwell when he was out late at night, and receive him in his terrible condition. It was she who was most often in Branwell's company. It has often been said that her novel, *Wuthering Heights*, reads like the dream of an opium-eater; and there is little doubt that, while the atmosphere of the book was her very own—the pure, wild, rain-swept atmosphere of her beloved, purple-black moors—the ugly human drama—the story of Heathcliff and Catherine—was Emily Brontë's weird and powerful interpretation of the ravings of her drug-sodden brother.

And there can be no doubt, though little has ever been said about it, that the reception of *Wuthering Heights* was a keen disappointment in those last months of Emily Brontë's life. She and Anne had been generously sympathetic with Charlotte's successes—Thack-

THE VALLEY OF THE SHADOW 75

eray's praise, the letters and books and reviews that were always coming from 65 Cornhill, the drafts of £100 that followed each new edition. Even Anne's *Tenant of Wildfell Hall* was in a second edition—that very commonplace and orthodox presentment of the evils of drink and profligacy, as the poor little sister had seen them daily before her eyes. And Emily's book— a work of immature but extraordinary genius, written with a woman's very heart-blood, a work " surcharged with a sort of moral electricity "—had been a failure. The people who had read it were shocked by it—that was all.

When Emily was ill, Charlotte read aloud a notice in the *North America Review*, very uncomplimentary to all three of " the Bells." Emily smiled, " half amused and half in scorn," as she listened. It must have been at this very time she wrote her last passionate lines, beginning:

> "No coward soul is mine,
> No trembler in the world's storm-troubled sphere
> I see Heaven's glories shine,
> And faith shines equal, arming me from fear." [1]

To the outside world Emily Brontë has always been an enigma. It is difficult to explain the silent obstinacy which prevented her from acknowledging that she was ill. She would see no " poisoning doctor "; she would accept no help. Slowly and painfully she would dress herself, and even doggedly take up her sewing, to the very last hours of her life. Yet, " I think Emily seems the nearest thing to my heart in this world," wrote Charlotte when her sister was dying. In her own home Emily was passionately loved.

" Day by day, when I saw with what a front she met suffering, I looked on her with an anguish of wonder and love. I have seen nothing like it; but, indeed, I have never seen her parallel in anything. Stronger than a man, simpler than a child, her nature stood alone."

[1] *Selections from the Literary Remains of Ellis and Acton Bell.*

They buried her in the church aisle, with her mother and sisters and the "hapless brother." One of the group of mourners at the grave was the bulldog, Keeper. He had joined the little procession, and "walked alongside of the mourners" and into the church, and with them he had stayed quietly till the last words of the burial service had been read. Then he had gone home, to lie disconsolate outside Emily's bedroom door. He would never lie on the hearthrug again with Emily and her German books, Emily's thin arm about his bulldoggy neck.

In that very December 1848, the famous article on *Vanity Fair* and *Jane Eyre* appeared in the *Quarterly*. The writer—anonymous at the time, but afterwards known to be Miss Rigby, who became Lady Eastlake—hazarded the unpleasant suggestion that if *Jane Eyre* were by a woman, it must be a woman who "for some sufficient reason has long forfeited the society of her sex." For some time her publishers kept back the *Quarterly*, but at last they were obliged to let Charlotte Brontë see it. She took it very quietly. "The lash of the *Quarterly*," she wrote back, "however severely applied, cannot sting. Currer Bell feels a sorrowful independence of reviews and reviewers." She kept the *Quarterly* to herself, knowing that it would only "worry papa." She was always very careful to tell the parson just enough of her literary successes to please, without exciting him. She was at work on another novel, to be called *Shirley;* but she never talked much about her writing, and father and daughter were at this time thinking only about Anne.

Anne was as docile and reasonable as Emily had been unflinching—"the patientest, gentlest invalid that could be."[1] The winter and spring passed wearily. Ellen Nussey and their old schoolmistress, Miss Wooler, did what they could. Far-away doctors were consulted, remedies suggested and tried, respirators and warm soles for little shoes were sent by post, and plans were made for change of air when the weather

[1] Mrs. Gaskell's *Life*.

THE VALLEY OF THE SHADOW

should be warmer. "I long to do some good in the world before I leave it," Anne wrote to Ellen Nussey. "I have many schemes in my head for future practice—humble and limited, indeed, but still I should not like them all to come to nothing . . . but God's will be done." And in this mood she wrote the pathetic lines that were to be her last, beginning:

> "I hoped that with the brave and strong
> My portioned task might lie,
> To toil amid the busy throng
> With purpose pure and high."[1]

In May, Charlotte took luxurious lodgings at Scarborough, and on May 24th a sad little cavalcade left the parsonage, the "little sister" carried downstairs to the open chaise by Charlotte and Ellen Nussey. They spent a night at York, and Anne was carried into the Minster, to look and listen her last. At Scarborough they hired a donkey-chair, and drove her on the sands, and she held the reins herself, afraid lest the donkey should be over-driven. On Sunday, the 27th of May, they dissuaded her from going to church; but in the evening the three women, from the windows of that Scarborough lodging, watched in silence a most glorious sunset over the sea, the castle and cliff standing out against the crimson of the setting sun, "the distant ships glittering like burnished gold."

And next day Anne Brontë died in their arms. "Give Charlotte as much of your company as you can," she whispered to Ellen Nussey, and to Charlotte herself, "Take courage, Charlotte! take courage!"

Anne Brontë was buried at Scarborough. A week or ten days later Charlotte returned home alone. The parson, old Tabby, and Martha met her at the door. The dogs—Emily's "Keeper" and Anne's little "Flossy" —seemed "in strange ecstasy." In their doggy minds her return only heralded the others.

And Charlotte? She went into the old dining-room, where they had walked up and down so many times,

[1] *Selections from the Literary Remains of Ellis and Acton Bell.*

with arms about each other's waists. The dear old partnership was dissolved. She shut herself in; all by herself she faced "*the agony that was to be undergone.*"

"Solitude, remembrance, and longing" were to be her companions, night and day.

CHAPTER XII

THE ZENITH

WITH an almost superhuman effort Charlotte Brontë finished writing *Shirley*. About two-thirds of the novel had been written before Branwell died; then, while Emily and Anne were ill, the manuscript had been laid aside. Now, sitting alone in the parsonage, Charlotte took it up, and began writing at the chapter that she has called "The Valley of the Shadow of Death."

The novel was finished by the end of August. Early in September the manuscript was sent off to Messrs. Smith & Elder in London, and *Shirley*, in three volumes, was published on October 26th.

Jane Eyre had contained much that was autobiographic, but the plot of *Shirley* is laid among the scenes, and peopled with the men and women, known to Charlotte Brontë from her childhood up. The local colour and atmosphere are exact. The Yorke family are "almost daguerreotypes" of her old friends the Taylors of Gomersal; the "fighting gentry" are there to the life, exactly as they used to gather round the parsonage tea-table. And Shirley herself is Emily Brontë— Emily, as she might have been.

Charlotte hoped, since the incidents of the story were imaginative, that she might escape detection; but in this she was mistaken. A Haworth man in Liverpool read the novel, and guessed its authorship. He was quite sure it must have been written by somebody belonging to Haworth, and who in that village could have written it if not the parson's daughter, Charlotte?

THE ZENITH

The Haworth man wrote to the Liverpool papers, and the secret was out.

And so "Currer Bell," the sole survivor of the little trio "Bell & Co.," was at last discovered; and the London literary world was all agog when, in November, Charlotte was in London again, not this time at the old Chapter Coffee-house, but with the Smiths, who duly lionised her, and took her to see the sights of London—to her an "exciting whirl." She was very shy and nervous, and easily overtired. She said all the wrong things to Thackeray when he was asked to meet her at dinner, and she had an uncomfortable sensation that he must think her "fearfully stupid." The fact was, he puzzled her; she could never tell if he were in jest or earnest. She was more comfortable in Miss Martineau's society; and it is to Miss Martineau and Mrs. Gaskell that we owe the descriptions of this little literary lioness of 1849. In her deep mourning gown, Quakerlike in its simplicity, Charlotte Brontë looked an almost childlike figure among the Londoners. Her beautiful hair was smooth and brown, her face sensible and self-controlled, her wonderful eyes "blazing with meaning."

"I never saw the like," says Mrs. Gaskell about those eyes, "in any human creature." They made you, she says, forget that the face was plain; they arrested the attention; they attracted all those whom Charlotte Brontë herself would have cared to attract. And Mrs. Gaskell has paid a pretty tribute to the dainty fit of the shoes and gloves, the extreme smallness of the foot and hand—that little hand that lay in the palm of a friend "like the soft touch of a bird."

Shirley was well reviewed, and "went off" well, though the *Times* notice was so severe that hot tears fell on Charlotte's lap as she read it. And G. H. Lewes, who had been such a friendly critic to the unknown "Mr. Currer Bell," hurt Charlotte Brontë's sensibilities, now that he knew she was a woman, by his article, with all its banalities about the duties of womanhood, in the *Edinburgh Review*.

After all, her real triumph was at home, in Haworth. She confessed to Mary Taylor—out in New Zealand—that she had lived too long in seclusion to enjoy London society. She felt herself disqualified for it; she had become "unready, nervous, excitable"; she found herself either incapable of speech, or else given to talking vapidly. But at home she was the daughter of the venerable incumbent, the little châtelaine of the oblong stone parsonage, as well as a real live literary lady. "The Haworth people have been making great fools of themselves about *Shirley*," she wrote to Ellen Nussey; "they have taken it in an enthusiastic light." *Jane Eyre* and *Shirley* had been added to the library of the Mechanics' Institute at Keighley, and, of course, all the members wanted to read *Shirley* immediately. The villagers were delighted, and Martha, the parsonage maid, came home greatly excited. "Please, ma'am, I've heard such news! You've been and written two books, the grandest books that ever was seen!"

People began to come to Haworth from a distance for the chance of a glimpse of the author of *Jane Eyre* and *Shirley;* and John Brown, the sexton, pocketed half-crowns for pointing her out at church on Sundays. The Kaye-Shuttleworths drove over to call at the parsonage, to persuade her to visit them at the Lakes; and Lord John Manners and a brilliant house-party arrived at the parsonage, Lord John carrying a brace of grouse for the parson's table. Even the three curates—Mr. Smith, Mr. Grant, and Mr. Bradley—magnanimously forgave her for her treatment of them in *Shirley*. They seem, indeed, to have been rather flattered, and they certainly did not leave off coming to tea.

It must not be supposed that poor Mr. Weightman, of pleasant memory, will be found among the "Holyes" in any of Charlotte Brontë's novels. His successor, Mr. Smith—the Mr. Malone of *Shirley*—was no longer curate of Haworth when *Shirley* appeared in 1849. He had been promoted to another living shortly after Charlotte's return from Brussels, and since that time Mr. Brontë's coadjutor in the parish had been Mr. Arthur

THE ZENITH

Bell Nicholls. Mr. Nicholls was delighted with *Shirley*; for it may be remembered that, at the end of the novel, a Mr. Macarthey—the curate who succeeds Mr. Malone—is spoken of as one who "did as much credit to his country as Malone had done it discredit. . . . He laboured faithfully in the parish; the schools, both Sunday and day schools, flourished under his sway like green bay-trees. Being human, of course he had his faults. These, however, were proper, steadygoing, clerical faults. The circumstance of finding himself invited to tea with a dissenter would unhinge him for a week; the spectacle of a Quaker wearing his hat in the church, the thought of an unbaptized fellow-creature being interred with Christian rites—these things could make strange havoc in Mr. Macarthey's physical and mental economy; otherwise he was sane and rational, diligent and charitable." [1]

Mr. Macarthey was avowedly drawn from the character of Mr. Nicholls; and when Mr. Nicholls sat himself down in his lodgings in Haworth village to read *Shirley*, his landlady "seriously thought he had gone wrong in his head, as she heard him giving vent to roars of laughter, and even clapping his hands and stamping on the floor."

It had been more than once rumoured that there was, or might well be, an attachment between the parson's clever daughter and the "Christian gentleman" who had laboured faithfully for so many years as curate of Haworth, and who seemed to have no ambition to move on elsewhere. But Charlotte Brontë had always laughed at the rumour, and denied it. "Who gravely asked you whether Miss Brontë was not going to be married to her papa's curate?" she wrote to Ellen Nussey in 1846. "I scarcely need say that never was rumour more unfounded."

As the years went by, mentions of Mr. Nicholls crop up in her letters—slight, indeed, but always as of one at hand, ready to do any service required of him. It was Mr. Nicholls who was ready to take up his abode

[1] *Shirley*, Chapter xxxvii.

at the parsonage and look after the parson when Charlotte was away from home. When she is flaunting demurely in the big Babylon, and writes such dutiful little letters to "papa" at home, there is always a message to Mr. Nicholls, as well as to old Tabby and Martha and the dogs. The years 1850 to 1852 were, in spite of poor health and depressed spirits, "Currer Bell's" most brilliant years; and Mr. Nicholls, by birth a proud and taciturn Scot, was only a poor curate with one hundred a year. Even so late as 1852 Charlotte Brontë was not thinking of marrying her father's curate; and certainly Mr. Brontë was not thinking of it. All the old man's social and intellectual ambitions, so often and so cruelly disappointed, seem at last to have been satisfied in "my daughter"—my daughter's genius, my daughter's novels, and my daughter's publishers. He carefully preserved every literary notice; he accepted, with a pathetic mixture of pride and humility, the little attentions that reached him through her celebrity. He enjoyed Lord John Manners's grouse, and he browsed to his heart's content among the boxes of books that came from Cornhill. With an old man's dread of any interference with his daily habits of life, he was feverishly anxious that Charlotte should see more society. He pressed her to accept invitations, assuring her he should get on nicely with Tabby and Martha and Mr. Nicholls. Mrs. Gaskell thought it sounded very depressing when Charlotte wrote, in autumn: "Papa and I have just had tea; he is sitting quietly in his room, and I in mine. Storms of rain are sweeping over the garden and churchyard. As to the moors, they are hidden in thick fog." And it was still more depressing when she wrote, in winter: "London and summer are many months away. Our moors are all white with snow just now, and little redbreasts come every morning to the window for crumbs."

But it must be remembered that Mrs. Gaskell and Charlotte Brontë were two absolutely different natures. Charlotte Brontë's genius had grown and flowered in a hard and stony soil, under a stormy sky; it had no

THE ZENITH

affinity with the gay window-boxes of a London season. She enjoyed, in a sort of a way, her little fortnights in June—a debate in the Commons; a sight of the Great Duke, at last, face to face; her nervous little wit-combats with the Titan Thackeray; her graver encounters with Lewes, whom she forgave, because he was so like Emily! She enjoyed her visits to the Kaye-Shuttleworths and to Miss Martineau at the Lakes, and to Mrs. Gaskell in Manchester. She looked back with romance on her little tour to Edinburgh and Abbotsford with the Smiths. But she was always glad to get back to her father and the intense silence of the parsonage; to her own little realm of pen and ink, and the boxes of new books sent so regularly from Cornhill.

While she was in London in 1850, she sat to Richmond for her portrait. It was Mr. George Smith's gift to her father; and with it came another portrait, a wonderful head of the Great Duke, Charlotte's lifelong hero. Both portraits gave enormous pleasure at the parsonage. The parson's letter of thanks to Mr. Smith was in itself a work of early Victorian art. Old Tabby was more critical: she did not think the artist had done justice to her young lady; but the other portrait was the living image of "the master"!

Towards the end of 1850, Messrs. Smith & Elder republished *Wuthering Heights* and *Agnes Grey*, with a memoir of her sisters by Charlotte Brontë. She had already begun to write her third novel, *Villette;* but the revision of these stories, and the writing of that most pathetic of memoirs, had been a "sacred duty"— as she calls it—but also a difficult and painful task. It had brought back vividly the days when the sisters were together under the parsonage roof. Sad and restless, Charlotte did not seem able to get on with *Villette*. She was always taking it up, and putting it aside again. "There was no one to whom to read a line, or to whom to ask a counsel. *Jane Eyre* was not written under such circumstances, nor were two-thirds of *Shirley*."[1]

[1] Mrs. Gaskell's *Life*.

Early in 1851 another suitor appeared at Haworth parsonage. Mr. James Taylor—a Scotsman, a clever man, managing clerk to Messrs. Smith & Elder, and the man who had sat up half the night to read *Jane Eyre*—came all the way to Haworth to prefer his suit. Mr. Brontë liked Mr. Taylor; it would apparently have satisfied his sense of the fitness of things if Charlotte had become Mrs. James Taylor. The old parson even told his daughter that he had made up his mind, if she married, "to give up housekeeping and go into lodgings." But, alas! "friendship, gratitude, and esteem" were forthcoming; but Charlotte confessed that in the presence of Mr. James Taylor her "veins ran ice." And so Mr. Taylor received his *congé*, and shortly afterwards the firm sent him away to manage a branch of their publishing business in Bombay.

Perhaps the month in London that followed on this little romance was the most brilliant month in Charlotte Brontë's life. For it was the year of the great Exhibition; and she had provided herself with a white lace cloak to wear over her black satin gown, and a bonnet with a lining of pink drawn silk. And it was the year of Thackeray's lectures in Willis's Rooms; and she found herself at the second of the lectures, in the "cream of London society." And Thackeray himself—with duchesses and countesses all round him—met "Currer Bell" at the door, and took her up to where his mother was sitting—"the fine, handsome, young-looking old lady." And Lord Carlisle and Monckton Milnes introduced themselves in whispers to Miss Brontë, as "Yorkshiremen"; and after the lecture was over, the cream of London society made a pathway for "Currer Bell" as she walked out, "all in a tremble!"

The Crystal Palace in Hyde Park—that "mixture of a genii palace and a mighty bazaar"—fairly bewildered her, though she walked about it on Sir David Brewster's arm. She saw Rachel, the great French actress; and it was "terrible, as if the earth had cracked deep at her feet and revealed a glimpse of hell." Service at the

THE ZENITH

Spanish Ambassador's chapel, with Cardinal Wiseman in his robes and mitre, seemed to her "impiously theatrical"; but d'Aubigné, the French Protestant preacher, had moved her strangely. "It was half sweet, half sad, and strangely suggestive to hear the French language once more." On her way home she stayed with the Gaskells in Manchester, and spent a whole day in choosing a shawl as a present for Tabby. And when Miss Wooler came to pay a visit at the parsonage—the parson had for years carried on a patriarchal flirtation with Miss Wooler—the company of her old schoolmistress seemed to Charlotte, even after all the society of the Babylon, "like good wine."

But the winter of 1851–52 was one of sickness, loneliness, and terrible depression. Such sad little milestones marked the road! Poor old "Keeper," quite toothless and fond only of the doorstep in the sun, died in December. "Flossy" missed his drowsy company. *Villette* lagged; Charlotte wanted strength and spirits to write it.

In June Charlotte visited Scarborough and Anne's grave, all alone. That summer the parson was seriously ill, and all the time Messrs. Smith & Elder were pressing her for the new novel. They wanted to advertise "Currer Bell's New Work" for the publishing season. When, in September, the Great Duke died, Charlotte scarcely noticed the passing of her hero; her letters are only a cry of "I don't get on. . . . I feel fretted—incapable—sometimes very low."

It was Mr. Brontë who insisted on a visit from Ellen Nussey; and his prescription acted like magic. "After her friend's departure," says Mrs. Gaskell, "she was well enough to 'fall to business,' and write away, almost incessantly, at her story of *Villette*." It was finished, and in the hands of her publishers, in November 1852. "I said my prayers when I had done it," she wrote.

Charlotte Brontë would have liked *Villette* to be published anonymously; she wanted to have "the sheltering shadow of an incognito." But of course that was impossible. The book was delayed a little while to give

86 THE BRONTËS

Mrs. Gaskell's *Ruth* a start; and Charlotte arranged to go to London in January, on a visit to the Smiths, and to correct the proofs of *Villette* while she was there.

But something happened in that December, between the sending off of the manuscript of *Villette* and the January visit to the Smiths in London, that was to change the whole current of this woman's life—or what remained of it.

CHAPTER XIII

THE PASSING OF CURRER BELL

CHARLOTTE BRONTË had suspected for some time that Mr. Nicholls "cared for her." One evening he had come to tea at the parsonage; and after tea in the study Charlotte had, as usual, returned to her own sitting-room. She heard the study-door open, and thought the curate was going away; but instead there came a tap at her own door, and "like lightning it flashed upon me what was coming." This man, ordinarily so statue-like, whom she had known merely as "papa's curate" for so many years, now stood before her trembling with a passion he could no longer control. His words and his manner moved her as she had never in her life been moved before. And yet, a hundred doubts and fears assailed her. She did not love him; his feelings, his tastes, his principles were not congenial to her. There was "a sense of incongruity." At the moment she could only entreat him to go away, and wait till to-morrow for her answer. "I think I half led, half put him out of the room."

The poor old parson was terribly upset when Charlotte told him what had happened. He had been ill, and the veins stood out on the old man's forehead "like whipcord." Charlotte was frightened. She hastened to assure her father that she would not think of marrying Mr. Nicholls. She wrote a refusal, and sent it down to the curate's lodging in the village.

THE PASSING OF CURRER BELL

And so Mr. Nicholls sent in his resignation; and Mr. Brontë, very angry, began to look out for another curate; and Charlotte, very ill at ease, went off to correct the proofs of *Villette* in London.

And *Villette*, when it appeared at last, in that February of 1853?

Villette " was received with one burst of acclamation."

The reviews simply poured into Charlotte Brontë's lap as she sat quietly in the house of her kind friends. For the moment all literary London was at the little feet of " Currer Bell."

" I am only just returned to a sense of the real world about me," wrote George Eliot, " for I have been reading *Villette*. . . . There is something almost preternatural in its power. . . . *Villette* . . . *Villette* . . . have you read it ? "

The months that followed the publication of *Villette* were very harassing months to Charlotte and the parson and Mr. Nicholls. The parson was implacable. He saw no reason why Charlotte should marry at all; but if she did, it ought to be " very differently." The author of *Jane Eyre* and *Shirley* and *Villette* would be " throwing herself away " by marrying a curate with £100 a year; and Charlotte was making £500 for the copyright of each novel! It was ridiculous. The two men were scarcely on speaking terms; and, indeed, Mr. Nicholls had grown so morose that nobody in Haworth could make anything out of him. *Villette* appeared in February, and Mr. Nicholls left Haworth in May. In the interval he must have got hold of and read this novel by the woman he loved, of which all the world was talking. With what feelings did he follow the story that it told ? He went about his parochial duties to the last maintaining a stony reserve. It was entirely his own fault, he told the churchwardens, that he was leaving the parish; he blamed nobody, and he was very sorry to go. Perhaps the thing that most touched Charlotte's heart was the curate's care of Anne's dog, " Flossy." Flossy waddled off regularly to Mr. Nicholl's lodgings in the village, and to the last day of his sojourn among them Mr. Nicholls took Flossy with him on his customary daily walk. Charlotte could not but admit that this was a man whose attachments were few, whose feelings were strong and deep, running like " an underground stream in a narrow channel." When the day came for him to go, their parting was a painful one. And no sooner had Mr. Nicholls gone than " papa " discovered that he could not get on at all with Mr. de Renzi, the new curate.

Towards the end of September Mrs. Gaskell paid that visit to the parsonage of which she has left so wonderful a word-picture. The two women, novelists and friends, had much to say to each other ; and Mrs. Gaskell, who was in the secret, did what she could with Mr. Brontë— " a most courteous host "—and with some other people too, Monckton Milnes among them, to further Mr. Nicholls's interests. " The great conqueror Time," she says, was to do the rest. The winter had passed uncomfortably and anxiously, when, one day in April, the old man relented. Another curacy was found for Mr. de Renzi, and Mr. Nicholls was asked to come back. " In fact, dear Nell," wrote Charlotte to her lifelong friend, " I am engaged."

Very quietly they were married, on June 29, 1854. Miss Wooler and Ellen Nussey arrived the day before the wedding. Everything had been arranged for the parson's comfort while they should be away. The honeymoon was to be spent in Ireland, among Mr. Nicholls's people ; and on their return the husband and wife were to take up their life together under the parsonage roof. Mr. Nicholls was quite satisfied to go on being " papa's curate " while the old man lived.

At the last moment the parson did not feel equal to the wedding ceremony. The Prayer-book was hastily consulted ; and Miss Wooler, " ever kind in emergency," on being assured no rubric was being broken, agreed to give her old pupil away.

. . . . .

It is allowed that *Villette* is more autobiographical than anything Charlotte Brontë wrote. " Lucy Snowe "

THE PASSING OF CURRER BELL

is very like the little woman whose life was so near its end when her book of "almost preternatural power" took London by storm. While she was writing her story, alone in the silent parsonage, Charlotte Brontë must have lived over again those two years in the Brussels *pensionnat*. It is all there, in those pages—the life of the *pensionnat*, the little world of human character around her, the outstanding personality of the "professor," the solitary days, the mental conflict, the bell of S. Gudule, the wooden grating of the confessional. She was determined that Lucy Snowe's life was to have no happy ending; her future was to be obscured.

"The sun passes the equinox; the days shorten, the leaves grow sere; but—he is coming.

"Frosts appear at night; November has sent his fogs in advance; the wind takes its autumn moan; but—he is coming."

And the reader knows that Paul Emanuel will never come.

But almost as Currer Bell was writing these last words of her *Villette*, there had come the tap to her door; the passionate avowal of a love that was close at hand, that would not die. Was it a wise step? Would it be a happy marriage? It was not brilliant, certainly; the literary Londoners would not understand it at all. Charlotte herself must have known that marriage with Mr. Nicholls—if she did her duty as a curate's wife—meant the passing of " Currer Bell."

We must take her own word for it that she was happy in her choice: " I trust I feel thankful to God for having enabled me to make what seems a right choice, and I pray to be enabled to repay as I ought the affectionate devotion of a truthful, honourable man."

Her letters to " dear Nell " speak with a shy tenderness of the new life and the new master; but with the new year (1855) the little wife, always so delicate, fell ill. The doctor "assigned a natural cause." Martha tried to put heart into her mistress by talking of the baby that was coming; but it was too late. " I dare say

I shall be glad some time," she would say, " but I am so ill—so weary."

Her last pencil notes were to her "own dear Nell." Her last words were to the husband who bent over her with murmured prayer. " Oh," she whispered, " I am not going to die, am I ? He will not separate us ; we have been so happy ! "

. . . . .

Mr. Brontë and his son-in-law lived together in the parsonage for six years longer, till Mr. Brontë died in 1861. Then Mr. Nicholls returned to Ireland, and the living of Haworth passed into other hands.

There is a railway station at Haworth now, and the old place is much changed. The church has been rebuilt ; the parsonage has been " improved " ; the very moors are not what they were when Currer, Ellis, and Acton Bell walked on them with their arms about each other's waists. But Haworth will always be known as the home of the Brontës.

CHRONOLOGY

Patrick Brontë, b. 1777.
Maria Branwell, b. 1783.
Their marriage, Dec. 29, 1812.
Patrick Brontë's curacies:—
 Wethersfield, Essex, 1806.
 Wellington, Salop, 1809.
 Dewsbury, Yorkshire, 1809.
 Hartshead-cum-Clifton, 1811.
Maria Brontë, b. 1813.
Elizabeth, b. 1814.
Charlotte, b. April 21, 1816.
Patrick Branwell, b. 1817.
Emily Jane, b. July 30, 1818.
Anne, b. Jan. 17, 1820.
Patrick Brontë's publications, 1811, 1813, 1815, 1818.
Removal to Haworth, Feb. 1820.
Death of Mrs. Brontë, Sept. 15, 1821.
Children at Cowan Bridge, 1824-1825.
Charlotte at Roehead, 1831-1832.
At Roehead again, 1835-1838.
Branwell in London, 1835.
Emily at Roehead, 1835.
Anne at Roehead, 1835-1837.
Emily at Halifax, 1836.
Henry Nussey proposes to Charlotte, 1839.
Charlotte and Anne as governesses in private families, 1839-1841.
Mr. Bryce proposes to Charlotte, 1839.
Branwell at Broughton-in-Furness, 1840; at Sowerby Bridge, 1840; at Luddenden Foot, 1841.
Charlotte and Emily at Brussels, 1842.
Death of Aunt Branwell, 1842.
Charlotte returns to Brussels, 1843-1844.
Anne and Branwell at Thorp Green, 1845.
Poems by "Currer, Ellis, and Acton Bell" published 1846.

Jane Eyre published 1847.
Wuthering Heights and *Agnes Grey* published 1847.
Tenant of Wildfell Hall published 1848.
Charlotte and Anne in London, 1848.
Death of Branwell, Sept. 24, 1848.
Death of Emily, Dec. 19, 1848.
Death of Anne, May 28, 1849.
Shirley published 1849.
Charlotte's visits to London, 1849, 1850, 1851, 1853.
James Taylor proposes to Charlotte, 1851.
Villette published 1853.
Charlotte's marriage with Mr. Nicholls, June 29, 1854.
Charlotte's death, March 31, 1855.
Death of Patrick Brontë, June 7, 1861.

REFERENCES

The Life of Charlotte Brontë, by Mrs. Gaskell. (Smith, Elder, & Co., 1900.)

Charlotte Brontë and Her Circle, by Clement K. Shorter. (Hodder & Stoughton, 1896.)

Charlotte Brontë. A Monograph, by T. Wemyss Reid. (Macmillan & Co., 1877.)

Life of Charlotte Brontë, by Augustine Birrell. (Walter Scott, 1887.)

Emily Brontë, by Mary F. Robinson. (Allen & Co., 1883.)

The Brontë Family, with Special Reference to Patrick Branwell Brontë, by Francis A. Leyland. (2 vols.; Hurst & Blackett, 1886.)

The Brontës in Ireland; or, Facts Stranger than Fiction, by Dr. William Wright. (Hodder & Stoughton, 1893.)

The Works of Charlotte Brontë and her Sisters. (7 vols. Haworth Edition; Smith, Elder, & Co.)